Be
Filled
With the
Spirit

Other Zondervan publications by this author —

The End of This Present World
God's Plan for the Future
When Loved Ones Are Taken in Death

Be Filled With the Spirit

Lehman Strauss

ZONDERVAN PUBLISHING HOUSE
OF THE ZONDERVAN CORPORATION
GRAND RAPIDS, MICHIGAN 49506

To Bill and Margaret Pew,
whose generous philanthropies have
made possible a wider distribution
of God's Word.

Library of Congress Cataloging in Publication Data

Strauss, Lehman.
　Be filled with the Spirit.

　1.　Holy Spirit.　　I.　Title.
BT121.2.S87　　　231'.3　　　76-11829

Fourth printing　June 1977
ISBN 0-310-33072-6

BE FILLED WITH THE SPIRIT

Contents

Preface 9
1. Which Spirit? 11
2. The Fact of the Holy Spirit 19
3. The Function of the Holy Spirit (Part One) 27
4. The Function of the Holy Spirit (Part Two) 39
5. The Figures of the Holy Spirit 53
6. The Filling With the Holy Spirit 69
7. The Faction Between the Holy Spirit and the Flesh 89
8. The Fruit of the Holy Spirit 101
9. The Future Ministry of the Holy Spirit 117

Preface

You have honored me by picking up this small volume on a subject that we need to know about. I am hopeful that you will exercise the patience to read it through. If you are an average Christian, there is within your heart a yearning after an above-average spiritual experience.

The lost emphasis on the person and work of the Holy Spirit is a sad feature in religious life. Believers new in the faith are to be pitied because they are not hearing what the Bible teaches about the Holy Spirit. Too often, experience is given preference over truth. The Christian who has been taught correctly and clearly on this major biblical subject cannot but be profoundly thankful to God.

Wherever I go in my travels, I meet people who ask questions about the Holy Spirit. To me this is an encouraging sign, because the correct understanding of the ministry of the Holy Spirit is basic to right Christian living. It is axiomatic that one must believe right in order to behave right. However, most of us believe much better than we behave.

It is almost trite to say that the church is beset by problems, and the chief reason for the problems is the fact that the individual Christian has problems. You see, the church is people; the church is not a denomination, nor an organization, nor a building. The church is people, and the people who make up the church have problems.

I am convinced that the solution to these problems is found, not in a doctrine, but in a Person, and that Person is the Holy Spirit. I am not overstating it when I tell you that no subject in the matter of religion should engage our powers more than the subject I have undertaken in this book. If the biblical teachings on the person and work of the Holy Spirit were expounded faithfully in our pulpits today, most of the confusion and unchristian behavior would disappear.

The questions being asked today come from many persons who are sincere Christians, including pastors. This tells me something, namely, that many Christian schools which train young men for the ministry are not fulfilling their solemn responsibility in a concern that should be given top priority. Because we have neglected the blessed Holy Spirit, the church today lacks the power of the first-century church.

I am persuaded that we must approach our study with a right attitude toward Holy Scripture, for it is in this Book of all books one finds the truth. The person who insists upon giving first place to experience is off the track, thereby showing that he has a defective attitude toward the Word of God. If what the Bible teaches is not the one true source of inerrant information about the Holy Spirit, you might just as well close this book now and consider the price you paid for it a waste. But if, on the other hand, you are not certain in your own mind about the source and soundness of the contents of the Bible, then I must urge you to read on.

I know that you, my brothers and sisters in Christ, join with me in magnifying the Scriptures as the Word of God. But even we who love God's Word must be careful lest we allow tradition or denominational background or family influence to usurp the authority of the Word itself.

For the moment I beseech you, with unshackled thinking, to join with me to study seriously and ponder prayerfully some basic beliefs about the person of the Holy Spirit.

LEHMAN STRAUSS

Be
Filled
With the
Spirit

Chapter 1

Which Spirit?

WHICH SPIRIT?

The church's choicest blessing is being peddled in caricature in pulpits and religious bookstores across America. I refer to the Third Person of the Trinity, the blessed Holy Spirit. In this age of religious activism I am greatly concerned over the irreverent treatment He receives from some preachers and writers.

TESTING THE SPIRITS

A solemn passage of Scripture says, "Beloved, believe not every spirit, but try the spirits whether they are of God: because many false prophets are gone out into the world" (1 John 4:1). Apparently there are those who cannot discern between the Holy Spirit of the Bible and other "spirits." Included in those other "spirits" are "the spirit of man" (1 Cor. 2:11), "the spirit of the world" (1 Cor. 2:12), "the spirit that now worketh in the children of disobedience" (Eph. 2:2), and "that spirit of antichrist" (1 John 4:3).

On more than one occasion the Pharisees in Christ's day could not discern the spirits. When our Lord cast out demons from those who were possessed, the Pharisees said He did it

11

by the power of the prince of the demons (Matt. 9:32-34), an evil spirit. But He told them that He did it "by the Spirit of God" (Matt. 12:28). They could not tell the difference.

Many in our day have no more discernment than did those Pharisees. A similar confusion is in our midst; however, the situation is in reverse. The work of other "spirits" is being attributed to the Holy Spirit. Excitement, shouting, hand-raising, and words such as "amen" and "hallelujah," coming from persons in a public gathering, are attributed to the Holy Spirit. But one can hear and see the same behavior coming from people in their show-business performances or in a sports arena. A friend of mine asked me to be his guest at the Alabama-Notre Dame football game in the 1975 Orange Bowl. There was continuous shouting, hand-raising, and excitement from the moment of the kickoff to the final gun. And from some fans in the stands behind me I heard two "hallelujahs" and one "amen." Which spirit?

One of the gifts of the Holy Spirit is the "discerning of spirits" (1 Cor. 12:10), that God-given ability to distinguish clearly whether the assertions and actions of a person are prompted by the Holy Spirit or some other spirit. This gift of "discerning of spirits" is important "because many false prophets are gone out into the world" (1 John 4:1). Paul warned in 2 Timothy "that in the last days perilous times shall come" (3:1). Then he listed some of the perils, among them being those persons "having a form of godliness, but denying the power thereof." And to this he added, "from such turn *away*" (2 Tim. 3:5), not turn *to*.

But I find myself asking, Why are so many people following other "spirits" and not the Holy Spirit? Now, the people I refer to are religious, meeting-going, Bible-carrying persons. They seem to lose restraint and self-control at the sound of the name "Jesus" or "Amen" or "Praise the Lord." I do not have all the answers to my own question. But I do know that much of the religious activism I am seeing has no biblical basis.

Note once more Paul's word to Timothy. The apostle described this peril as "having a form of godliness" (2 Tim.

3:5). The word *form* means that the peril follows a pattern. The Revised Version uses the word *pattern* both here and in 2 Timothy 1:13.

THERE IS A COUNTERFEIT

Some people have not learned that Satan is not an innovator, but an imitator. He is a copyist, but his copies are counterfeit. When Jesus warned His own to beware of Satan's emissaries, He said, "Beware of false prophets, which come to you in sheep's clothing, but inwardly they are ravening wolves. Ye shall know them by their fruits . . . " (Matt. 7:15, 16). Other "spirits" produce their fruits, and the Holy Spirit produces His fruit. The tragedy lies in the fact that too many persons can discern neither the spirits nor the fruits.

Read carefully the following divinely inspired words from the pen of the apostle Paul:

> For such are false apostles, deceitful workers, transforming themselves into the apostles of Christ. And no marvel; for Satan himself is transformed into an angel of light. Therefore it is no great thing if his ministers also be transformed as the ministers of righteousness; whose end shall be according to their works (2 Cor. 11:13-15).

The early church was experiencing the peril of the counterfeit. The demon of darkness appeared then as an angel of light, causing Paul no little concern and consternation. He said to those believers, "But I fear, lest by any means, as the serpent beguiled Eve through his subtilty, so your minds should be corrupted from the simplicity that is in Christ" (2 Cor. 11:3). There can be no doubt that Satan is behind the religious activity of the other "spirits."

It seems quite clear that there were in Corinth men who were preaching a brand of Christianity which was not God's. They regarded themselves as very special people, superspiritual. Tragically, the Corinthians gave them a hearing; therefore Paul exposed them for what they were, false apostles masquerading as Christian witnesses. Paul added that all who are guilty of such deeds will have an end corresponding to their deeds (11:15). But much damage had already been

13

done. An evil spirit had penetrated the church in Corinth, adding to the already existing Corinthian confusion. The believers there did not "try the spirits." They were long on the gift of tongues, but short on the gift of "discerning of spirits."

Women, will you be patient with me while I stress a point here? Verse 3 says, "The serpent beguiled Eve through his subtilty." Now please note 1 Timothy 2:14, which says, "And Adam was not deceived, but the woman being deceived was in the transgression." Now, I did not write those words; God the Holy Spirit is their Author. But I do believe they are apropos at this point in our study. Why did Satan come to Eve first rather than to Adam? Obviously he believed he could deceive her with greater ease than he could deceive Adam. In this he was correct. And again the Scriptures give us the reason. You will find it in Peter's First Epistle, where he writes, "Likewise, ye husbands, dwell with them according to knowledge, giving honour unto the wife, as unto the weaker vessel . . ." (3:7). God says the wife is the *weaker*, and therefore more susceptible to Satan's subtilty, an easier prey for the spirits.

An acquaintance of mine, a medical doctor, was treating a Spanish-speaking husband and wife. This couple were devotees of Mary Baker Eddy and her religious system known as Christian Science. The doctor had prayed that the Holy Spirit might make it possible for him to witness about Jesus Christ and His great salvation. So that he might be prepared, the doctor worked hard on improving his Spanish. On one of his visits, the prayer was answered as the Holy Spirit opened the door for a witness.

During the course of the conversation, the woman said, "Doctor, how do you know Mary Baker Eddy is not right? She uses the Bible."

"Yes," replied the doctor, "but she uses the Bible on condition that you be guided by her 'key to the Scriptures.' If Mary Baker Eddy is correct, what about the millions who lived and died during almost nineteen hundred years before Mary Baker Eddy was born?" The woman could not grasp

14

the point the doctor was making. Suddenly her husband's face became aglow, and he cried, "I see it now!" The Holy Spirit had taken those Scriptures the doctor used in his witness, and at once the truth was grasped. Both the man and his wife received Christ that day as their Savior and Lord. That man discerned the spirits.

I am not putting down the woman. Her role in this life is a vitally important one. I love and respect my wife, and I have a high regard for her judgment (after all, she did choose me to be her husband), but we both believe what the Bible teaches. She is the weaker vessel. But then, there have been times when her wise counsel held me in check, and I thank God for her.

Had Mary Baker Eddy yielded to the Holy Spirit and not been led by another spirit, she never would have started the evil system that has blighted millions. Yes, there is "another spirit" (2 Cor. 11:4), but that "spirit" is not the Holy Spirit.

What About Miracles?

One of the blights upon the church today is the emphasis upon the spectacular, that which smacks of the miraculous, the supernatural. Everything connected with genuine Christianity is supernatural, including the Bible, the virgin birth, resurrection, and ascension of Jesus Christ, the New Birth, and much more. What many cannot see is that Satan can imitate gifts and miracles. The miracle of God performed through Moses and Aaron was duplicated by the magicians of Pharaoh (Exod. 7:8-12). An evil spirit matched a miracle of the Holy Spirit.

Robert K. Massie, in his book *Nicholas and Alexandra*, relates how a miracle deceived the czar and czarina of Russia and ultimately destroyed their empire.

Federovna, the German wife of Czar Nicholas II, gave birth to a son, the heir to the Russian throne. In a matter of weeks, the doctors discovered that the infant had hemophilia, an incurable blood disease. The members of the royal family were greatly disturbed by the doctors' discovery, because to them the child's death would be disastrous.

But a greater tragedy occurred. In Russia at that time was a wicked man, a religious mystic by the name of Gregory Rasputin. Some recall him as "the mad monk of Russia." In desperation the czar and his czarina sought the powers of Rasputin for the healing of their son.

Every time Rasputin said prayers over the sick child, there would be a definite improvement. After each session with the child, Rasputin would remind the parents that the child could live only as long as they followed his instructions. Because of their love for the child and their dreams for the future of the empire, they bowed to Rasputin's every request.

With a word the wicked Rasputin could obtain the appointment or dismissal of any government official. Those who were under his influence and control he caused to be appointed; those who were not he had dismissed. It did not take long for this demon-possessed evil man to have the entire Russian government under his control.

The bitter fruits that followed plague civilization to this day. The royal family was murdered, followed by civil war and the takeover by the Communists. One government official who survived that disaster said, "Without Rasputin, there could have been no Lenin." Czar Nicholas II and his Czarina Federovna were deceived through a miracle. They could not discern the spirits.

After I had finished speaking at an evening service in a church in New Jersey, a woman came rushing at me with fire and fight in her eyes. She said, "Well, I conclude you don't believe that God performs miracles today." She was wrong: I do believe God performs miracles today. I *know* He does. I can disprove the claims of those persons who insist that God is not performing miracles. Any Christian who has walked in unbroken fellowship with the Lord over a long period of time can testify to a miracle-working God. Missionaries can testify to God's miracle-working power in both providing for them and protecting them. I am saying what the Bible says, namely, there are spirit forces, possessed of superhuman power, which can produce miracles. These forces are at work in our midst today.

"Beloved, believe not every spirit, but try the spirits whether they are of God: because many false prophets are gone out into the world" (1 John 4:1).

A Discerning Church

Have you read recently the words of commendation from our Lord about the church at Ephesus? The church in that city was not perfect. It had a major weakness: Jesus said, "Thou hast left thy first love" (Rev. 2:4). But in spite of its weakness, the believers there were possessed of great strength in that they could discern the spirits.

Jesus said, "Thou canst not bear them which are evil: and thou hast tried [i.e., tested] them which say they are apostles, and are not, and hast found them liars" (Rev. 2:2). Apparently the assembly in that great city did not have all the gifts, but they did have the gift of "discerning of spirits." It was this gift that spared them from the Corinthian confusion.

It is interesting that Paul had warned the elders at Ephesus to be on their guard against a false spirit. "And from Miletus he sent to Ephesus, and called the elders of the church." He said to them, "For I know this, that after my departing shall grievous wolves enter in among you, not sparing the flock. Also of your own selves shall men arise, speaking perverse things, to draw away disciples after them" (Acts 20:17, 29, 30). We must conclude from the testimony of Jesus that Paul's warning paid off.

The more serious problems among Christians could be corrected if only we would be led by the Holy Spirit and not some other spirit.

Study Questions

1. Why is the gift of "discerning the spirits" important today?
2. What was the nature of the "superspiritual" problem in the church at Corinth?
3. How does Satan imitate the works of the Holy Spirit?

17

Chapter 2

The Fact of the Holy Spirit

THE FACT OF HIS PERSONALITY

"I got *it!* I got it!" Mrs. B—— screamed as she came running into the house.

"What did you get?" her husband asked.

"Harold, I got the Holy Ghost. It's that new chrismatic [she meant *charismatic*] experience the girls have been talking about."

"Martha, you left the motor running in the car and there is an energy crisis" was Harold's only response.

Mrs. B—— was still on "cloud nine," so she yelled back at her husband, "Harold, once you get *it* you'll stop worrying about a little gasoline."

Right or wrong? Let us look into God's Word, and then you come to your own conclusion.

The subject under discussion in this chapter is basic and foundational. It is not some deep theological concept that should be confined to a seminary classroom, but one that every Christian should know.

There are millions of professing Christians who have stood in churches to recite the "Apostle's Creed." This well-known and historic creed includes the statement, "I believe in the Holy Ghost." Now, many of those persons who memorized and recited the creed have devoted neither time nor effort to finding out who the Holy Spirit is.

If you will examine closely that creed, you will see that it contains ten articles describing the person and work of our Lord Jesus Christ, but only two brief statements about the Holy Spirit. I am not finding fault with those men who put together the articles of faith, nor will I criticize what they said. My one criticism is against what they did *not* say: they said very little about the Holy Spirit. This observation on my part I believe to be a fair one.

If we believe in and confess the fact of the Holy Spirit, it follows that we must accept the fact of His personality. To deny His personality is to deny His real existence. It is an easy matter to fall prey to the psychological fallacy that the Holy Spirit is an "it," a mere power, an energy, a force.

A few hundred years after the death of Christ, a heretic named Arius spread the wild idea that the Holy Spirit was merely the "exerted energy of God." This false concept continued and thereby laid the groundwork for modern Unitarianism. Today there are millions who, through ignorance or unbelief, deny the personality of the Holy Spirit. It is not uncommon to hear the blessed Third Person of the Holy Trinity referred to as "an influence from God." This erroneous teaching does not make sense.

The habit of referring to the Holy Spirit as an impersonal "it" might be the result of the translation in the King James Version of the Bible. Note three verses:

> The Spirit itself beareth witness with our spirit, that we are the children of God" (Rom. 8:16).
>
> Likewise the Spirit also helpeth our infirmities: for we know not what we should pray for as we ought: but the Spirit itself maketh intercession for us with groanings which cannot be uttered (Rom. 8:26).
>
> Searching what, or what manner of time the Spirit of Christ which was in them did signify, when it testified beforehand the sufferings of Christ, and the glory that should follow (1 Peter 1:11).

In all three verses, the neuter pronoun *it* or *itself* is used in reference to the Holy Spirit. There is an explanation for this. In the Greek language, which is the original language in which the New Testament was written, there is what is called "grammatical gender." This means that the object in the sentence can be either masculine, feminine, or neuter, that is, a "he," a "she," or an "it." This is not limited to the Greek language; other languages have in them the grammatical gender.

In the Greek language, the word for spirit is *pneuma,* a neuter noun. The translators, adhering strictly to syntax, gave to us the neuter pronoun. Grammatically this is acceptable. However, had the translators given to us the real sense of the word, they would not have referred to the Holy Spirit as an "it." The Spirit of God is always "he," "his," "him," or "himself."

Even though the word *spirit (pneuma)* is neuter, it is incorrect to make reference to the Holy Spirit as a mere power or influence. For example, read some of our Lord's references to the Holy Spirit:

> And I will pray the Father, and he shall give you another Comforter, that he may abide with you for ever (John 14:16).
> But the Comforter, which is the Holy Ghost, whom the Father will send in my name, he shall teach you all things, and bring all things to your remembrance, whatsoever I have said unto you (John 14:26).
> But when the Comforter is come, whom I will send unto you from the Father, even the Spirit of truth, which proceedeth from the Father, he shall testify of me (John 15:26).
> Nevertheless I tell you the truth; It is expedient for you that I go away: for if I go not away, the Comforter will not come unto you; but if I depart, I will send him unto you. And when he is come, he will reprove the world of sin, and of righteousness, and of judgment (John 16:7, 8).
> Howbeit when he, the Spirit of truth, is come, he will guide you into all truth: for he shall not speak of himself; but whatsoever he shall hear, that shall he speak: and he will shew you things to come. He shall glorify me: for he shall receive of mine, and shall shew it unto you (John 16:13, 14).

Three essential elements are common to personality — *intellect, emotion,* and *will* — and all three are claimed for the Holy Spirit.

With the intellect, a person can think and know and understand. The Holy Spirit possesses this attribute. He has a mind (Rom. 8:27), and He is able to teach. Jesus said, "He shall teach you all things, and bring all things to your remembrance, whatsoever I have said unto you" (John 14:26). "He will guide you into all truth" (John 16:13). The Holy Spirit knows and teaches because He has the capacity of intellect, one of the necessary attributes of personality.

His emotional capacity, or sensibility, is further proof of His personality. He can be grieved (Eph. 4:30), quenched (1 Thess. 5:19), and resisted (Acts 7:51) — facts which would be meaningless if He were not a person. The Holy Spirit prays (Rom. 8:26), a statement that would not make sense if He were a mere influence and not a person.

His will is shown in His capacity and determination to bestow gifts upon men, "dividing to every man severally as he will" (1 Cor. 12:11). When Paul wanted to go into the province of Asia to preach, he was forbidden by the Holy Spirit (Acts 16:6, 7). The Holy Spirit calls men into the gospel ministry and sends them forth to preach (Acts 13:1-4). Because of this, it does not make sense to say that the Holy Spirit is nothing more than an influence or a power emanating from God. He is a person.

THE FACT OF HIS DEITY

The Holy Spirit is not a person merely; He is a divine person, He is God. The Word of God presents clearly the truth that the Holy Spirit, along with the Father and the Son, possesses all of the essential attributes of deity.

Eternality is an essential attribute of deity. The Father is eternal (Deut. 33:27), the Son is eternal (John 1:1), and the Spirit is eternal (Heb. 9:14). There is an eternal relationship between the three persons in the Godhead, thus the Spirit is placed on the same level as the Father and the Son. The baptismal formula is in "the name of the Father, and of the

Son, and of the Holy Ghost'' (Matt. 28:19). The apostolic benediction follows this same formula: ''The grace of the Lord Jesus Christ, and the love of God, and the communion of the Holy Ghost, be with you all. Amen'' (2 Cor. 13:14). The relationship of the three persons in these passages indicates both personality and deity. It would be completely unnatural to regard the Spirit as being less than the Father and the Son.

Omniscience is an essential attribute of deity. The Latin prefix *omni,* meaning ''all,'' and *science,* meaning ''knowledge,'' give to us our English word *omniscience,* which means ''all knowledge.'' If there were anything God does not know He would cease to be God. The Holy Spirit possesses omniscience— ''For what man knoweth the things of a man, save the spirit of man which is in him? even so the things of God knoweth no man, but the Spirit of God. Now we have received, not the spirit of the world, but the spirit which is of God; that we might know the things that are freely given to us of God'' (1 Cor. 2:11, 12). Jesus said to His disciples, ''He shall teach you all things'' (John 14:26). He is called ''the Spirit of knowledge'' (Isa. 11:2) and ''the Spirit of truth'' (John 14:17).

Omnipotence is an essential attribute of deity. The word *omnipotence* means all (unlimited) power. Only God has unlimited power. The major evidence of divine omnipotence is witnessed in the creation of the universe. ''In the beginning God created the heaven and the earth'' (Gen. 1:1). The word *God* is the translation of the Hebrew word *Elohim,* a plural noun suggesting the plurality of persons in the Godhead. While all three persons in the Holy Trinity were active in creation, certain aspects of creation are attributed to the Holy Spirit: ''The spirit of God moved upon the face of the waters'' (Gen. 1:2). The Spirit was active in the creation of man: Elihu said, ''The spirit of God hath made me, and the breath of the Almighty giveth me life'' (Job 33:4). The Holy Spirit played a vital part in imparting life to all creation, thereby demonstrating His deity and omnipotence.

Omnipresence is an essential attribute of deity. To be

23

present in all places is an attribute that only God may possess. The psalmist, writing by divine inspiration, said, "Whither shall I go from thy spirit? or whither shall I flee from thy presence? If I ascend up into heaven, thou art there: if I make my bed in hell, behold, thou art there. If I take the wings of the morning, and dwell in the uttermost parts of the sea; Even there shall thy hand lead me, and thy right hand shall hold me" (Ps. 139:7-10). David found comfort in the continuing presence of the Holy Spirit.

The Spirit dwells at the same time in the hearts of all believers (John 14:17; 1 Cor. 3:16; 6:19, 20). In December 1927 I was born again, saved. That day the Holy Spirit entered my body, and He has been with me now for almost fifty years. On many occasions my work for God has taken me away from my family for periods of time. But whenever those times of separation from my loved ones occurred, I have found strength and comfort in the fact that the Spirit of God is just as near to them as He is to me. It is the consistent teaching of the Word of God that the Holy Spirit is God.

The names and titles of the Holy Spirit support the fact of His Deity. He is called —

> My Spirit (Gen. 6:3)
> The Spirit of God (2 Chron. 15:1)
> The breath of the Almighty (Job 32:8)
> The Holy Spirit (Ps. 51:1)
> The Spirit of the LORD . . . the Spirit of wisdom, understanding, counsel, might, knowledge (Isa. 11:2)
> The Spirit of the Lord GOD (Isa. 61:1)
> The Spirit of life (Rom. 8:2)
> The Spirit of Christ (Rom. 8:9)
> The Spirit of power (Rom. 15:13)
> The Spirit of our God (1 Cor. 6:11)
> The Spirit of the living God (2 Cor. 3:3)
> The Spirit of the Lord (2 Cor. 3:18)

These many titles of the Holy Spirit, with their different connotations, speak eloquently of the majesty of His person and work. They tell us that He is equal in greatness and glory with both the Father and the Son. Christians who have an intelligent comprehension of just who the Spirit is have made a good start in their Christian experience. To believe in the full-orbed personality and deity of the Holy Spirit makes sense. It is the only tenable position of orthodox Christians.

The moment a person becomes saved, his body becomes the temple of the Holy Spirit. This Holy Person moves in, clothing Himself with our bodies. Therefore, we must get acquainted with Him, cultivate personal and intimate fellowship with Him. He is God, and we need Him every moment of every day. He wants to direct us and thereby save us from making mistakes. His ministry in and through us is indispensable to successful and victorious living.

In view of all I have said thus far, some of the brethren will accuse me of depreciating Christ. One good brother wrote, "Any movement, teacher or teaching which exalts the Holy Spirit is not of the Holy Spirit! The Holy Spirit always exalts Christ." There is some truth in that statement. Our Lord Jesus did say concerning the Holy Spirit, "He shall glorify me" (John 16:14). However, giving the Holy Spirit His rightful place according to the Scriptures will never depreciate Christ. Read through the four Gospel records and you will find not less than nineteen references to the Holy Spirit given by Christ Himself.

Satan is an imitator, a counterfeiter. One of his devices is to offer a forgery so close to the genuine that even believers can be deceived. And I know of no doctrine more fraudulently imitated than the doctrine of the Holy Spirit. The modern charismatic movement is an example of satanic deception; the devotees of this sect are victims of a delusion. The misleading of their minds results, not from ignorance of the person and work of Christ, but because they are confused and befuddled about the ministry of the Holy Spirit.

It is true that the Holy Spirit does not exalt Himself, but it is equally true that the Word of God establishes Him in the exalted position of a member of the Godhead, coequal with the Father and the Son. The Corinthian charismatic catastrophe resulted from blindness concerning the office and operations of the Holy Spirit. And for the same reason, the Corinthian problem remains with us today.

I have observed that unless there is a return to the plain sense of scriptural teaching on the person and work of the Holy Spirit, we can expect a growing confusion. The very heart of a truly spiritual life is in the teaching of the Word of God. Some of our experiences may add up to nonsense, but the Bible does make sense. When the sincere and Spirit-taught student searches the Scriptures, he discovers that the truth sets him free from all extrabiblical ideas. The Lord Jesus said, "If ye continue in my word, then are ye my disciples indeed; And ye shall know the truth, and the truth shall make you free" (John 8:31, 32).

Study Questions

1. What was the wrong idea Arius held about the Holy Spirit, and how is it manifested today?
2. Explain why the pronoun *it* is improper in reference to the Holy Spirit.
3. What characteristics of personality are possessed by the Holy Spirit?
4. What attributes of God the Father are possessed by the Holy Spirit?
5. Name some titles given to the Holy Spirit in Scripture.

Chapter 3

The Function of the Holy Spirit

PART ONE

HIS FUNCTION IN CREATION

In most instances the work of creation is attributed to God without a distinction of persons in the Godhead. However, there are those Scriptures which relate creation to each individual member in the Holy Trinity. In most passages dealing with creation, God the Father is given the prominent place, but it is clearly stated in Scripture that both the Son and the Holy Spirit had a definite part in the creative work. The passages that follow are but a few of many.

Genesis 1:1 — "In the beginning God created the heaven and the earth." The word *God* is the translation of *Elohim*, a genuine plural. It is not merely the plural of majesty and greatness, but a genuine numerical plural, indicating the three persons in the Godhead. Therefore the work of creation is not that of one person only, but of all three persons. This is supported by the next verse.

Genesis 1:2 — "And the spirit of God moved upon the face of the waters." I reject totally the idea that the statement merely means that a wind fanned the face of the waters. It is not a mere energy emanating from God, but the person of the Holy Spirit Himself. We should not be averse to insisting upon attributing Genesis 1:2 to a definite creative work of the Holy Spirit.

Psalm 33:6 — "By the word of the Lord were the heavens made; and all the host of them by the breath of his mouth." The word translated *breath (ruach)* is the same word translated *spirit* in Genesis 1:2. It is not some spirit which is a mere potency or power emanating from God, not a mere principle, but the person Himself. In this connection see also Psalm 104:30.

Isaiah 40:12-14 — "Who hath measured the waters in the hollow of his hand, and meted out heaven with the span, and comprehended the dust of the earth in a measure, and weighed the mountains in scales, and the hills in a balance? Who hath directed the spirit of the Lord, or being his counsellor hath taught him? With whom took he counsel, and who instructed him, and taught him in the path of judgment, and taught him knowledge, and shewed to him the way of understanding?" Here the Holy Spirit is described as the One who, in His creative work, needed no counsel, no instruction, no one to assist Him in any way.

Job 26:13 — "By his spirit he hath garnished the heavens." This is a reference to the Holy Spirit's giving to the heavens their beauty. This could refer to the Milky Way or to the stars in general.

Job 33:4 — "The spirit of God hath made me, and the breath of the Almighty hath given me life." Here is a direct reference to the Spirit's work in the creation of man. This verse, along with the above passages, supports the activity of the Holy Spirit in creation, thereby attesting His deity.

His Function in Inspiration

The well-being of the church is threatened today as never before in her history. The church is at the crossroads. The major issue revolves around the Bible, and the decision must be made as to whether we will listen to the voices of Satan and men, or heed the Word of God.

Every religion has some basis of authority on which its followers believe and behave. For the Christian the authority is the Bible, called "the oracles of God" (Rom. 3:2; Heb. 5:12), the "Scriptures" (2 Tim. 3:16; 2 Peter 1:20; 3:16), "the Word of God" (John 10:35; Heb. 4:12). How this Book of all books came to us is important. Is it the product of the mind of man, or did it come from God?

The doctrine of inspiration is constantly being thrust into the forefront of discussion. Religious leaders do not hesitate to tell us what we may and may not believe about inspiration. Frankly, I am convinced that the Bible should be permitted to tell us exactly what kind of a book it is and how it came to be. I reject totally those conclusion of men which run counter to the Bible's testimony to its own inspiration.

In my use of the term *inspiration* I mean that the Holy Spirit superintended the human writers so that they wrote without error exactly what He wanted them to write. By this supernatural guidance the very words, not merely the concept in the original manuscripts, were inspired. The Bible is not merely a witness to the Word of God, nor does it merely contain the Word of God; it is in its entirety the very Word of God, *infallible* and *inerrant*. The Bible is the product of God the Holy Spirit, therefore I could never speak too highly of it. I recognize that human penmen were His instruments, and that each of the sixty-six books in the Bible has its own human scribe, but God the Holy Spirit is its Author.

Second Samuel 23:2 — "The spirit of the LORD spake by me, and his word was in my tongue." Here David bears witness to the fact that the Holy Spirit spoke to him and through him, thereby testifying that he was aware of the work of the Holy Spirit in inspiration.

Matthew 22:41-44 — "While the Pharisees were gathered together, Jesus asked them, Saying, What think ye of Christ? Whose son is he? They say unto him, the Son of David. He saith unto them, How then doth David in spirit call him Lord, saying, The LORD said unto my Lord, Sit thou on my right hand, till I make thine enemies thy footstool?" In this passage, along with Mark 12:36, Christ Himself testified clearly to the function of the Holy Spirit in inspiration when He quoted Psalm 110:1.

Acts 1:16 — "Men and brethren, this scripture must needs have been fulfilled, which the Holy Ghost by the mouth of David spake before concerning Judas, which was guide to them that took Jesus." Here Peter quotes Psalm 41:9, penned by David, but attributed in its origin to the work of the Holy Spirit.

Acts 28:25, 26 — "And when they agreed not among themselves, they departed, after that Paul had spoken one word, Well spake the Holy Ghost by Esaias the prophet unto our fathers, Saying, Go unto this people, and say, Hearing ye shall hear, and shall not understand; and seeing ye shall see, and not perceive." Paul, when in Rome, quoting Isaiah 6:9, 10, stated emphatically that the prophet Isaiah received his message from the Holy Spirit.

In the above references, as in other New Testament passages (see Heb. 3:7; 10:15, 16), witness is borne to the inspiration of the Old Testament by the Holy Spirit.

Second Timothy 3:16 — "All scripture is given by inspiration of God, and is profitable for doctrine, for reproof, for correction, for instruction in righteousness." Paul's view of the inspiration of the Scriptures finds perfect agreement with what the Lord Jesus taught in Matthew 5:17, 18 and John 10:33-35. The Greek term Paul used *(theopneustos)* means breathed out from God, or God-breathed. The Scriptures are the product of the Holy Spirit, the creative Breath of God. The distinctive feature of Christianity is its unique Textbook which is the work of the Holy Spirit.

HIS FUNCTION IN REVELATION

Now we consider a subject of vital importance, namely, the Holy Spirit as the Revealer of truth. It is not uncommon to hear someone ask, How does God speak to man today? We who believe that God is the Creator of all things believe also that He has a plan whereby He would communicate to His creatures. When God created man, He made a being with intellect, the kind of creature to whom He could communicate. Communication between God and man is reasonable.

The means of *revelation* have varied with the passing of time.

God revealed Himself first in creation.

Psalm 19:1-3 — "The heavens declare the glory of God; and the firmament sheweth his handiwork. Day unto day uttereth speech, and night unto night sheweth knowledge. There is no speech nor language, where their voice is not heard."

Romans 1:20 — "For the invisible things of him from the creation of the world are clearly seen, being understood by the things that are made, even his eternal power and Godhead; so that they are without excuse." These passages seem to state quite clearly that there was a time when God revealed Himself through the universe He created, a revelation sufficient to condemn the heathen world.

Then, too, God revealed Himself through the spoken word. Without the aid of written documents, God spoke vocally directly to man. The Book of Job, which is possibly the oldest written record to man, was revealed by God to the writer of the book; the revelation was in words so clear and concise that Job and his companions could understand them. In like manner God spoke directly to Moses (Exod. 19:9). When Acts 28:25 is compared with Isaiah 6:9, 10, it is evident that the communication from God to man was the function of the Holy Spirit in a voice audible and understandable. Revelation, then, is one of the mighty and miraculous functions of the Holy Spirit.

None of the writers of Scripture could be true prophets or true apostles without having received their revelation from the Holy Spirit. "For the prophecy came not in old time by the will of man: but holy men of God spake as they were moved by the Holy Ghost" (2 Peter 1:21). David testified, "The spirit of the LORD spoke by me, and his word was in my tongue" (2 Sam. 23:2). Ezekiel also testified that his revelation was the work of the Holy Spirit (Ezek. 2:2; 8:3; 11:1).

Likewise the revelation to the New Testament writers came through the ministry of the Holy Spirit. The Lord Jesus assured His disciples that "the Holy Ghost, whom the Father will send in my name, he shall teach you all things, and bring all things to your remembrance, whatsoever I have said unto you" (John 14:26). "He will guide you into all truth . . . and he will shew you things to come" (John 16:13). From these references, along with others, it is clear that the revealing of truth to the writers of both the Old and New Testaments was the work of the Holy Spirit.

But the question many are asking today is, Does God give special and specific revelation today as He did in Old Testament history and in New Testament times? Or, is the Holy Spirit revealing new truth today? In seeking an answer to these question: we must exercise care not to confuse *revelation* with *illumination*. Man needs guidance, but guidance does not require some additional revelation from God. This brings us to our next thought.

HIS FUNCTION IN ILLUMINATION

In biblical studies on the work of the Spirit, three words are employed — *inspiration, revelation,* and *illumination.* When we speak of inspiration we have in mind one phase of the Spirit's work, namely, the production of the books that make up the Bible. His ministry of inspiration is a completed work; He is not now inspiring people to write more Scripture. When we speak of revelation we have in mind the means and methods whereby the Holy Spirit conveyed His message to men; He revealed His message in creation, through an audible voice, in dreams, visions, and trances. Revelation, like inspiration, is a completed work. God is not now giving additional revelation.

Self-styled prophets and prophetesses, astrologers and witches might claim new revelations, but they do not come from God the Holy Spirit; their source is some other spirit. In the 1950s the modern charismatic movement arose in America. Its rapid rise can be attributed to the relating of experiences, hearing voices, and seeing visions. Its followers claim to have received new revelations from God. But these experiences cannot be attributed to either the revelation or the illumination of the Holy Spirit.

The illuminating ministry of the Holy Spirit is inseparably linked with the Spirit's use of Scripture. His function in illumination is His work in the mind of the believer with regard to the meaning of Scripture. It cannot be stressed too strongly the fact of the Spirit's use of Scripture. The psalmist prayed, "Open thou mine eyes, that I may behold wondrous things out of thy law" (Ps. 119:18). The psalmist knew that there were treasures hidden in God's Word and that only the Holy Spirit could enlighten him; he could not by himself discover the hidden truth. It is humbling to our pride to be told that we cannot understand the Scriptures apart from the Spirit's illumination, but it is true nevertheless.

As we read and study the Bible we must pray for the Spirit's help. This function of the Spirit is easily neglected, though greatly needed. It is His personal ministry to show the individual Christian what the will of God is for him. The test is not in what people experience today, but in what the Scriptures say. God guides, sometimes through circumstances and events, but never contrary to what the Bible teaches. The Holy Spirit, then, is the Illuminator: He does not now reveal new truth, but He does cause us to understand the truth He has already revealed. "But as it is written, Eye hath not seen, nor ear heard, neither have entered into the heart of man, the things which God hath prepared for them that love him. But God hath revealed them unto us by his Spirit: for the Spirit searcheth all things, yea, the deep things of God" (1 Cor. 2:9, 10).

HIS FUNCTION IN INCARNATION

The word *incarnation*, which does not appear in the Bible, means "clothed with flesh." When God the eternal Son, who existed eternally in spirit form, took upon Himself a human body, He became incarnate, clothed with flesh. The Scripture says, "God was manifest in the flesh" (1 Tim. 3:16). The hymnwriter, speaking of the birth of Christ, wrote, "Hail the incarnate Deity!" When Jeremiah wrote prophetically of this forthcoming miracle, he said, "The LORD hath created a new thing in the earth, A woman shall compass a man" (Jer.

33

31:22). Describing this "new thing," Isaiah wrote, "A virgin shall conceive, and bear a son, and shall call his name Immanuel" (7:14).

How was this miracle in the Virgin's womb to be accomplished? This was the question that troubled Mary when the angel Gabriel told her that she would conceive and give birth to a son (Luke 1:30, 31). Mary's immediate response was "How shall this be, seeing I know not a man?" (Luke 1:34). Gabriel replied, "The Holy Ghost shall come upon thee, and the power of the Highest shall overshadow thee: therefore also that holy thing [or one] which shall be born of thee shall be called the Son of God" (Luke 1:35). Matthew wrote, "Now the birth of Jesus Christ was on this wise: When as his mother Mary was espoused to Joseph, before they came together, she was found with child of the Holy Ghost" (Matt. 1:18).

In these few Scriptures we have the record of the miraculous conception attributed to the work of the Holy Spirit. A mystery? Indeed, yes! But also a miracle! "The Word was God. . . . the Word was made flesh" (John 1:1, 14), not by natural generation, but by the supernatural operation of the Holy Spirit. Jesus said, "A body hast thou prepared me" (Heb. 10:5).

One liberal theologian wrote, "I cannot accept the idea of the virgin birth of Christ because it involves a biological impossibility." Such reasoning develops from one's refusal to accept the biblical teaching of the deity of the Holy Spirit and His function in inspiration.

Our Lord Jesus Christ was conceived (Matt. 1:20), born (Matt. 2:1), brought forth (Luke 2:7), made of a woman (Gal. 4:4) by the power of the Holy Spirit. The humanity of Christ came into existence creatively through the work of the Holy Spirit, therefore His humanity was without sin. This is the plain teaching of Scripture.

His Function in Regeneration

The Scriptures state clearly the fact that man is spiritually dead, lacking totally any spiritual life. "Wherefore, as by

34

one man [Adam] sin entered into the world, and death by sin; and so death passed upon all men, for that all have sinned" (Rom. 5:12). "In Adam all die" (1 Cor. 15:22). Christians, before their experience of regeneration, are declared to have been "dead in trespasses and sins" (Eph. 2:1). Sin and death are inseparably linked together. No unregenerated person has spiritual life, but is rather "alienated from the life of God" (Eph. 4:18).

The accomplishing of the believing sinner's salvation is called *regeneration*. Actually the word *regeneration* (Gr. *palingenesia)* appears only twice in the New Testament. The word itself means "a new order, a new beginning." The first appearance (Matt. 19:28) is used to describe the new order in the earth when Christ reigns during the Millennium. The second appearance is used in relation to our salvation, which is actually a new birth spiritually, a new beginning. Paul wrote, "Not by works of righteousness which we have done, but according to his mercy he saved us, by the washing of regeneration, and renewing of the Holy Ghost" (Titus 3:5).

Regeneration may be defined as that sovereign act of God whereby He imparts new life to the believing sinner. This life is God's own life, so that we are said to become "partakers of the divine nature" (2 Peter 1:4). A synonym for regeneration is the New Testament term "born again" (John 3:3-7). The word *again* (John 3:3, 7) should be rendered "from above," showing that the new birth is the act and achievement of God. Regeneration is "not of blood, nor of the will of the flesh, nor of the will of man, but of God" (John 1:13).

Particularly, regeneration is the work of the Holy Spirit. Jesus said to Nicodemus, "Except a man be born of water and of the Spirit, he cannot enter into the kingdom of God" (John 3:5). This verse has always been a difficult and debated passage of Scripture. What did our Lord mean by the use of the word *water*?

Water is used figuratively in the Bible in different ways, When it is used symbolically for *drinking* purposes it is a symbol of the Holy Spirit, as is stated clearly in John 7:37-39. When water is used symbolically for *cleansing* purposes it is a symbol of the Word of God, as is stated clearly in Ephesians 5:25, 26.

I see both the Word and the Spirit in Christ's statement in John 3:5. The Word of God is closely associated with regeneration. In fact, the Word of God is an indispensable means of the new birth. Peter wrote, "Being born again, not of corruptible seed, but of incorruptible, by the Word of God, which liveth and abideth for ever" (1 Peter 1:23). Paul wrote, "So then faith cometh by hearing, and hearing by the word of God" (Rom. 10:17). The Scriptures are not the only means of our regeneration, but they, like faith, are necessary in order for us to know what we must believe (see also James 1:18, 21).

The Word of God, energized by the Holy Spirit, produces regeneration. This miracle is not a process, but instantaneous. The new birth is a single, decisive act that never can be abrogated. No person who has been born again can ever be unborn. Our fellowship with God can be broken as a result of our sinning, but our relationship with God can never be broken. The Spirit's work in regeneration is both instantaneous and eternal.

HIS FUNCTION IN SANCTIFICATION

An important part in God's program for man is his *sanctification*. The doctrine of sanctification is one of the most discussed and debated among Christians. Our reason for the misunderstanding is the failure to grasp the meaning of the term. A basic error with some persons is their insistence that sanctification is associated merely with moral behavior; such a conclusion is incorrect.

The meaning of the verb *sanctify* (Gr. *hagiazo*) is "to set apart, to separate." Sanctification is that sovereign act of God whereby He sets apart a person, a place, or even an object for Himself and for the accomplishing of His purposes. Some of the things God has sanctified are a day (Gen. 2:3), a building (Exod. 29:44), and a mountain (Exod. 19:23).

All three persons in the Godhead are associated with sanctification in the Scriptures. But the Holy Spirit has a peculiar and particular ministry in the sanctification of the believer. At the time of the believing sinner's regeneration, the Holy Spirit enters his body, thereby sanctifying him, or setting him apart as God's possession and for God's purpose. All regenerated persons, without exception, are positionally sanctified, or indwelt by the Holy Spirit. The gift of the Spirit is never given discriminately, but rather to all saved persons. The person who does not have the Holy Spirit cannot possibly be saved, for "these be they who separate themselves, sensual, having not the Spirit" (Jude 19). "Now if any man have not the Spirit of Christ, he is none of his" (Rom. 8:9). When the Holy Spirit enters the body of the believer, that person becomes sanctified, or set apart.

Some of the clearest statements on the Spirit's incoming and indwelling are in 1 Corinthians. "Know ye not that ye are the temple of God, and that the Spirit of God dwelleth in you?" (3:16). "What? know ye not that your body is the temple of the Holy Ghost which is in you, which ye have of God, and ye are not your own?" (6:19). Now, those to whom the above verses were addressed were not spiritual and mature Christians. Some were carnal (3:1-3), others were living in gross sin (5:1-5), and still others were quarreling with each other so severely that they were entangled in legal battles (6:1). But with all their bad behavior they are said to be "sanctified in Christ Jesus, called to be saints" (1:2).

The verb *sanctified* means set apart, and the corresponding noun *saints* refers to all Christians who are God's set-apart ones. Positional sanctification is the state predetermined by God for every believer. "But we are bound to give thanks always to God for you, brethren beloved of the Lord, because God hath from the beginning chosen you to salvation through sanctification of the Spirit and belief of the truth" (2 Thess. 2:13).

It is this positional setting apart of the believer by the Holy Spirit which places him in the body of Christ. "For by one Spirit are we all baptized into one body . . ." (1 Cor. 12:13). The "body" is the church, the two terms being used inter-

37

changeably in Ephesians 1:22, 23. It is the baptizing work of the Spirit, which forms the church. Every saved person has been baptized by the Holy Spirit; Paul stated that *all* had the baptism, including the carnal Christians.

In the New Testament there are no exhortations or comments to believers to seek the baptism of the Spirit. The primary result of being baptized by the Spirit is that it makes us members of the body of Christ. There is no other way for one to become a member of Christ's church apart from the Spirit's baptism. Anyone may join a denomination or a local organized church, but the baptism of the Spirit is essential to effect the union with Christ. This is the believer's positional sanctification. Other aspects of his sanctification will be considered in a later chapter.

Study Questions

1. What was the Holy Spirit's function in creation?
2. What was the Holy Spirit's function in inspiration?
3. Distinguish between the work of the Holy Spirit in revelation and in illumination.
4. What was the Holy Spirit's role in the incarnation of Christ?
5. What is regeneration, and how does it involve the Holy Spirit?
6. Define positional sanctification and the Spirit's role in it.

Chapter 4

The Function of the Holy Spirit

PART TWO

One of the primary concerns of the ascended Lord appears to have been the necessary equipment for the survival of His church. He knew that she would be assaulted by the world, the flesh, and the devil, and for such a warfare supernatural gifts would be needed. Therefore, "When he ascended up on high, he led captivity captive, and gave gifts unto men" (Eph. 4:8). These gifts were to be dispensed by the Holy Spirit, and only under His control could they function successfully.

Five chapters in the New Testament speak of the spiritual gifts; Romans 12; 1 Corinthians 12, 13, and 14; and Ephesians 4. Perhaps the key chapters are the three in 1 Corinthians; these three constitute a major unit and should therefore be studied together. A clear understanding of this section of the epistle will do much to eliminate misunderstanding and confusion.

THE DISTINCTIONS WE MUST MAKE

In the Corinthian Church there was much misunderstanding about the gifts and their use. Paul was directed of the Holy Spirit to write so that the disorder and errors could be corrected; he wrote to rectify the abuse and wrong use of the gifts. This section on the gifts, 1 Corinthians 12–14, commences and closes with the key word *ignorant*. In addition to their carnality (3:1) they were ignorant. He began by telling them, "Now concerning spiritual gifts, brethren, I would not have you ignorant" (12:1), and then he completed his teaching on the gifts with the words, "But if any man be ignorant, let him be ignorant" (14:38). From these statements it is clear that Paul's purpose was to cure their misuse and abuse of the gifts. After instructing them, he reminded them that if they still did not understand, theirs was a willful ignorance. "If any man be ignorant, let him be ignorant." There was nothing further that Paul could do.

Now, lest we should be ignorant of the gifts and their use, there are some distinctions we must observe.

We must observe first a clear distinction between the Holy Spirit as a *Gift* and those *gifts* He dispenses. The former was the Father's Gift to the church at Pentecost fifty days after Christ's resurrection, so that the Spirit now dwells in the church corporately and in each believer individually. The gifts are those special abilities which God gives to each believer at the time of the believer's salvation experience. My point is that the gift is an ability, not an office which only a privileged few can ever occupy. For example, the gift of pastor-teacher is the ability God gives to a man to do the work of a pastor-teacher, so that the man who occupies the office most certainly should have the gift. In this instance the gift and the office are closely related. However, God might give this gift to a man to be used in some capacity other than in an organized church; students in a Christian school would need this shepherd-like care.

Another distinction should be made, namely, the discrimination between the *gifts* of the Spirit and the *fruit* of the Spirit. Fruit is a quality of character which should be produced in the life of every Christian. It is never a parceling out of the fruit such as one Christian's receiving love but not joy or peace. The ninefold cluster of fruit (Gal. 5:22, 23) is the product of the Holy Spirit's control over the life of the Christian, and it is to be manifested in every Christian. On the

40

other hand, the gifts are divided to the believers as the Holy Spirit determines. One Christian might be given one gift, and another will be given two or three. But no Christian is given all the gifts.

A third distinction to be recognized is the difference between a spiritual gift and a natural talent. Spiritual gifts function primarily in the realm of the Spirit, and natural talents in the natural realm. We Christians have natural talents as well as spiritual gifts; an unsaved person will have natural talents and abilities, but he will not have spiritual gifts. Natural talents may benefit the whole of mankind, but spiritual gifts are given primarily to the church. It is pathetic to observe unsaved persons trying to use natural talents to accomplish the work of God. We Christians must beware lest we attempt to do God's work in the energy of the flesh by means of our natural abilities. Spiritual gifts are given at the time of regeneration.

THE DIVERSITY OF SPIRITUAL GIFTS

"Now there are diversities of gifts, but the same Spirit. . . . and there are diversities of operations, but it is the same God which worketh all in all" (1 Cor. 12:4, 6). In these statements Paul seems to say that there are distinctions between gifts and a variety of ways of using the gifts. Each person receives his gift through the Holy Spirit, and it is God who gets credit for any accomplishments. "It is the same God which worketh all in all" (12:6). He is the "boss," and He alone can give the increase (3:6). On a farm one man may plow and prepare the soil, another may plant the seed, and still another may water it; but none of these men can take credit for having made the seed grow. All of us are servants, helpers, "labourers together with God" (3:9). We are merely exercising a God-given gift; therefore let us minimize our own importance and give all the glory and credit to God who gave to each his gift and enabled each to do his work for God.

In the church at Corinth tragic things were happening because there was ignorance on the part of those Christians as to the subject of gifts and their use. Paul's whole idea in

41

chapter 12 is to stress the unity of the church which is Christ's body. But in the church there can be unity without uniformity. Gifts differ as well as does the exercise of those gifts. Every gift was given through the Holy Spirit, and every one of them is designed to glorify God and not any individual member in the church. "But the manifestation of the Spirit is given to every man to profit withal" (12:7) — that is, for the common good of all, for the edifying of the whole.

In stressing the importance of unity in diversity, Paul uses the figure of the body and its members. Please note that it is more than an illustration: it is a figure that represents in reality the spiritual relationship which exists between Christ and the believer. That union is effected through the baptism in the Holy Spirit: "For by one Spirit are we all baptized into one body, whether we be Jews or Gentiles, whether we be bond or free; and have been all made to drink into one Spirit" (12:13).

From the figure of the body the apostle draws two basic lessons. The first is that there is one body, but many members (12:14). If the body is going to function properly, each member of the body must function properly. A body is healthy and efficient, only when each part of it is healthy and efficient. Poor eyesight or a toothache will affect the efficiency of the whole body. We must realize that we need each other (12:15-17), even those insignificant parts of the body which Paul calls the "more feeble" (weaker) and "less honorable" (12:22, 23). All are necessary for the good of the whole body.

The second lesson to be learned from the figure of the body is that no Christian is to despise his own gift. Diversity is normal and necessary if the body is to function properly. One member cannot say to another, "I have no need of thee" (12:21). On the other hand, neither can one member despise and deprecate himself because he cannot function as does another member of the body. "For the body is not one member, but many" (12:14). "If the foot shall say, Because I am not the hand, I am not of the body; is it therefore not of the body? And if the ear shall say, Because I am not the eye, I

42

am not of the body; is it therefore not of the body? If the whole body were an eye, where were the hearing? If the whole were hearing, where were the smelling? But now hath God set the members every one of them in the body, as it hath pleased him" (12:15-18). You see, the Christians at Corinth were magnifying the more showy and spectacular gifts to the extent that others in the assembly were made to feel that they were nothing and had no gift at all. Some of them were beginning to doubt that they were a part of the body. The admonition is: Do not despise another's gift, and do not despise your own gift.

THE DISTRIBUTION OF SPIRITUAL GIFTS

The Lord Jesus Christ is in heaven; He is no longer on this earth in a body. Therefore if He wants a particular task done for Him here on the earth, He needs someone to do it. If He wants His gospel told, He must find people to tell it. If He wants others taught, He must find a teacher to teach them. If He wants a book written, He needs a man to write it. Actually we Christians are the body of Christ, the voice to speak for Him, the hands to work for Him, the feet to carry His message and run His errands. And let us all be reminded that here is the great honor and privilege of being a Christian, that we are members of the body of Christ to carry on His work.

> He has no hands but our hands
> To do his work today;
> He has no feet but our feet
> To lead men in His way;
> He has no voice but our voice
> To tell men why He died;
> He has no help but our help
> To lead men to His side.

In order to accomplish His work on earth, the ascended Lord gave gifts to men. It is part of the Holy Spirit's function to distribute these gifts. Again I remind you that it was on this subject that the Corinthian believers were ignorant (12:1; 14:38). The confusion and disorder in the life of that assembly were the result of their misunderstanding of the gifts and

43

their distribution. Also, the gifts dispensed by the Holy Spirit were not to be confused with the natural talents and abilities that some had when they were born. Some children have a much higher intelligence quotient than do others. Paul is not speaking about those creative talents; he is speaking about gifts supernaturally bestowed upon a person when that person is born again.

The Word of God spells out what these gifts are: "He gave some, apostles; and some, prophets; and some, evangelists; and some, pastors and teachers; For the perfecting of the saints, for [unto] the work of the ministry, for the edifying of the body of Christ" (Eph. 4:11, 12).

Paul includes another list in his Epistle to the Romans: "Having then gifts differing according to the grace that is given to us, whether prophecy, let us prophesy, according to the proportion of faith; Or ministry, let us wait on our ministering; or he that teacheth, on teaching; Or he that exhorteth, on exhortation: He that giveth, let him do it with simplicity; he that ruleth, with diligence; he that sheweth mercy, with cheerfulness" (12:6-8).

Look now at the list Paul gives in 1 Corinthians: "For to one is given by the Spirit the word of wisdom; to another the word of knowledge by the same Spirit; To another faith by the same Spirit; to another the gifts of healing by the same Spirit; To another the working of miracles; to another prophecy; to another discerning of spirits; to another divers kinds of tongues; to another the interpretation of tongues" (12:8-10). "And God hath set some in the church, first apostles, secondarily prophets, thirdly teachers, after that miracles, then gifts of healings, helps, governments, diversities of tongues" (1 Cor. 12:28).

The important lesson we must learn is that all gifts are sovereignly dispensed by the Holy Spirit. A nationally known radio preacher told about a letter he received from a man. The writer of the letter claimed that he looked like Billy Graham, his voice sounded like Billy Graham's voice, and his gestures and mannerisms were very much like those of the famous evangelist. Because of these likenesses to Billy

Graham he thought he had the gift of an evangelist. The writer of that letter needed to learn the lesson we all must learn, namely, spiritual gifts are not to be sought by men. A man does not receive a spiritual gift because he desires it. Spiritual gifts are bestowed by the Holy Spirit apart from the will or the desire of the individual. The Holy Spirit distributes the gifts, "dividing to every man severally as He will" (12:11).

THE DISCOVERY OF SPIRITUAL GIFTS

Not all the gifts are necessarily given in every succeeding generation. By this I mean that some of the gifts were never intended to be exercised permanently throughout the church age. There were, then, temporary gifts such as the apostle and prophet, the gifts of healing, working of miracles, discerning of spirits, and speaking in tongues.

The gift of apostle and the gift of prophet, as these gifts relate to their respective offices, were temporary. The church was "built upon the foundation of the apostles and prophets" (Eph. 2:20). For nineteen hundred years God has been building upon that foundation. The superstructure has been added to steadily, and it is quite probable that the church is nearing completion. I can see how certain aspects of the work of the apostle and prophet might continue, but the office of each was obviously a temporary one. We do not need the office of an apostle or a prophet today, because we have the Scriptures. When missionaries and preachers carry God's Word to people to whom that Word has not come, they are doing the work of the apostle and the prophet; however, the offices *per se* were temporary. They are not being given today.

The gifts of healing, working of miracles, discerning of spirits, and speaking in tongues seem also to have been temporary gifts. It is true that the power to work miracles was given to the disciples (Matt. 10:1-8), and they did minister that power. However, there were times when they were not able to use the gift (Matt. 17:18, 19). Later, when our Lord sent out the Seventy, it was necessary that He give them the gift to perform miracles (Luke 10:1-9). After our Lord's

45

resurrection and the coming of the Holy Spirit, the gift of tongues was added. These all are *sign* gifts involving a miraculous demonstration of supernatural power. They were given temporarily to authenticate both the message and the messenger of God before the writing of the Scriptures was completed. God continues to perform miracles today; however, He is not bestowing those sign gifts to men. Gifts vary at different times according to the need.

There are three gifts that every Christian can have and use: *ministering* (which means helping or serving), *giving,* and *showing mercy* (Rom. 12:7, 8; 1 Cor. 12:28). There is no reason why every child of God cannot show his ability to help other people in need. Sharing our time and money, ministering kindness and mercy to those who are sick and less fortunate than ourselves, gives some indication of the extent of one's spirituality in God's sight.

The big question we all need answered is, "How can I discover my gift?" One thing we should not do is select a gift that we desire. Remember, the gift and the ability to use that gift efficiently must come from the Holy Spirit. A person might have the desire to be an evangelist or a pastor or a teacher; but he should not decide to exercise any gift if he has not received it from the Holy Spirit. Every Christian has some gift. I am not suggesting that all Christians are exercising the gift or gifts that the Holy Spirit has given to them; but each of us has at least one gift, for "the manifestation of the Spirit is given to every man to profit withal" (1 Cor. 12:7).

The following suggestions as to how a person might discover his or her gift have been helpful to me. I pass them along with the prayer that you will benefit from them.

First, there is the matter of *information*. Acquaint yourself with the gifts. Know what they are. Read again and again the three passages where the gifts are mentioned. Know which gifts were temporary and which are permanent. By being properly informed, you may discover that you have a gift of which you have been unaware. Then, too, you may discover that you have been using your gift while not aware of it.

My friend Leslie Flynn related an interesting incident. On

a trip around the world, a man and his wife arrived in Switzerland for a three-day stay. Checking tired into their hotel in late afternoon, they decided to eat in the hotel's dining room. The evening dinner was excellent but expensive. When they asked the waiter to add the cost to their hotel bill, he nodded consent, smiling in a knowing way.

To save money, the couple ate most meals out, but never had as fine food as that first evening. Receiving their hotel bill at the end of their stay, they noticed they had not been charged for that fine dinner. They learned, to their chagrin, that payment of advance reservations had included not only room, but meals as well. They could have eaten every meal for all three days in the hotel dining room at no extra cost.

Are you like that couple, unaware that you have something of worth that you are not using? Christian, we must all appear before the Judgment Seat of Christ to give an account of what we have done, or left undone (Rom. 14:10; 2 Cor. 5:10). Rewards will be given to us, or else withheld from us, for several reasons — including how faithfully we have exercised our gifts. Be informed! Know what the gifts are and which gift or gifts you have.

Second, there is the matter of *inclination*. What are your inclinations? What do you enjoy doing? What can you do well? This suggestion might raise a problem in the mind of some of you. Someone might ask, "How do you reconcile your suggestion with the teaching of Paul that the Holy Spirit sovereignly bestows the gifts upon whomever He chooses?" I am not saying that a person's inclinations are always a sure and safe guide to follow. It is possible that one's inclinations, desires, and aptitudes could be totally different from the gift the Holy Spirit has given. My desire for a certain gift along with my inclination toward the exercise of that gift will not guarantee it. In the final settlement of the matter, the assignment of the gift belongs to the Holy Spirit (1 Cor. 12:11; Heb. 2:4). We must leave the choice with Him. Our inclinations, however strong they might be, must never override the sovereignty of the Holy Spirit.

I am suggesting that God, being a God of order, might

relate our desires and inclinations to the gift He has given us. One's desires and inclinations just might indicate possession of a gift or gifts — not necessarily so, but possibly. Do you have the ability to teach, and do you enjoy teaching? Do you have a fine singing voice, and do you enjoy singing? Do you enjoy being a wife and becoming a mother, and are you successful in that dual role? Do you enjoy being merciful and helpful toward others, and do you find it easy to offer your services? I suggest that you consider your inclinations.

Third, there is the matter of *investigation*. We must explore and inquire. Naturally we commence with prayer: inquire first of God. "If any of you lack wisdom, let him ask of God, that giveth to all men liberally, and upbraideth not; and it shall be given him" (James 1:5). This is one of God's promises, and like all His promises, we can depend on it because we can depend upon Him. After all, we have only one go-around in this life, and it is a tragedy indeed when a Christian crosses the stage of human experience having failed to discover and develop the gift God gave to him. Inasmuch as everyone is given a gift, each of us must investigate as to what it is. "Ask and it shall be given you; seek, and ye shall find; knock, and it shall be opened unto you" (Matt. 7:7).

In pursuing the investigation, we should submit our minds to the counsel of older, more experienced, and discerning Christians. Others may detect our gift long before we ourselves are made aware of it. When I was nineteen years old, my pastor recognized my gift; at that time I did not know there was such a thing as a spiritual gift. The pastor continued to encourage me in several ways. Before I was twenty he arranged for me to preach, and I have kept busy at it for forty-five years. He was a real Barnabas, a "Son of Encouragement" (Acts 4:36 NIV). Barnabas recognized Mark's gift and never gave up on him (Acts 15:36-39). God has given this gift of encouragement to guide younger men.

But each of us must be prepared to face the possibility that others might recognize that we don't possess a gift we think we have. A proverb says, "Whoso boasteth himself of a false gift is like clouds and wind without rain" (Prov. 25:14). I once knew a young woman who thought she had the gift of singing, but I didn't know one person who had the gift of listening to her.

THE DEVELOPMENT OF SPIRITUAL GIFTS

The gift has been sovereignly bestowed by the Holy Spirit. Now we must use it to the fullest for God's glory. Whatever our gift or gifts, there are certain responsibilites on the part of the Christian if the gifts are to be used effectively and efficiently.

First, there is the *presentation*. Some might prefer to call it *dedication*. The apostle Paul wrote, "I beseech you therefore, brethren, by the mercies of God, that ye present your bodies a living sacrifice, holy, acceptable unto God, which is your reasonable service" (Rom. 12:1). Both the gift and the recipient of the gift must be yielded to the Lord: this is a necessary guideline for the development of the gifts. You will observe that immediately after Paul appeals to us to present our bodies, he takes up the subject of gifts (vv. 3-8). After we have presented and dedicated our bodies, we are to dedicate the gifts. This idea of commitment is not to be treated lightly. Remember that your gift is a sacred trust given by God when you were born again. It is not something to brag about or to show off. Paul asks, "For who maketh thee to differ from another? and what hast thou that thou didst not receive? now if thou didst receive it, why dost thou glory, as if thou hadst not received it?" (1 Cor. 4:7). The discovery of one's gift does not mark a person as someone special or uniquely spiritual. We will never use our gifts as God wants us to do without the control of the Holy Spirit. Yield yourself and your gift to God.

Second, there is the matter of *practice*. Discovering a gift should lead to its dedication, then to its development. In plain words, get going, work at it. The existence of a gift demands that it be exercised. Timothy was admonished concerning his gift; Paul said to him, "Neglect not the gift that is in thee, which was given thee by prophecy, with the laying on of the hands of the presbytery" (1 Tim. 4:14). Don't be careless about the gift God has given to you. Don't allow it to be dormant, but use it. What we don't use we lose. Work at your gift by giving yourself wholly to it. Diligent utilization of a gift produces increased effectiveness; failure to use it might render it useless. Paul told Timothy later, "Stir up the gift of God, which is in thee" (2 Tim. 1:6). Fan it into a flame! Possession of a gift demands its practice.

Third, there is the matter of *purpose*. In the exercise of his gift, each Christian must examine his motives. None of us has the right to use for selfish ends the gifts God has given to us. The apostle Peter wrote, "As every man hath received the gift, even so minister the same one to another, as good stewards of the manifold grace of God" (1 Peter 4:10). The exercise of our gifts should be in complete forgetfulness of self. We are "stewards" (caretakers, custodians) of the gifts, and "it is required in stewards, that a man be found faithful" (1 Cor. 4:2). Remember that the gifts are given for the common good of the whole body of Christ (1 Cor. 12:7). Since this is the purpose for the gifts' being given, we must therefore judge our motives in our exercise of them. The Lord Jesus warned that if we use our gifts selfishly we will lose the reward (Matt. 6:1-4). Our gifts are of no merit whatsoever if we fail to use them for the purpose God intended.

Fourth, there is the matter of *perseverance*. Perhaps some of you used your gifts in years past, but now are allowing those gifts to lie unused. If the hidden talents and buried treasures were recovered and put to work for God, we might witness a revival unprecedented in the church's history. But I fear there are too many Christians like Demas who, "having loved this present world" (2 Tim. 4:10), are allowing their gifts to remain unused. Beloved, we can't blame God for the lack of gifted workers. Christ gave the gifts to the church, and the Holy Spirit has distributed them faithfully, but too many selfish, self-centered Christians have quit. Never forget that once God gives a gift, He never takes it back, "for the gifts and calling of God are without repentance" (Rom. 11:29).

"And let us not be weary in well doing: for in due season we shall reap, if we faint not" (Gal. 6:9). The Lord Jesus said, "Be thou faithful unto death, and I will give thee a crown of life" (Rev. 2:10).

Study Questions

1. Distinguish between the "gift of the Spirit" and spiritual gifts.
2. Distinguish between the gifts of the Spirit and the fruit of the Spirit.
3. Why is there such diversity of spiritual gifts?
4. How are spiritual gifts related to natural talents and acquired abilities?
5. What gifts can every Christian have and use?
6. How does a Christian discover his particular gift or gifts?
7. How does a Christian develop a spiritual gift?

Chapter 5

The Figures of the Holy Spirit

As the student of the Bible becomes conversant with its language, he discovers that various figures of speech are employed, such as parables, metaphors, similes, types, emblems, and symbols. A symbol is a representation standing for or calling up something spiritual or moral. When a number of words are used to describe the same thing, we think of them as emblems or symbols. In this present study we will examine six figures of speech used in the Word of God, all of which describe the person and work of the Holy Spirit.

THE DOVE

The most familiar passage of Scripture which speaks of the dove as a symbol of the Holy Spirit is associated with our Lord's baptism. "And Jesus, when he was baptized, went up straightway out of the water: and, lo, the heavens were opened unto him, and he saw the Spirit of God descending like a dove, and lighting upon him: and lo a voice from heaven, saying, This is by beloved Son, in whom I am well pleased" (Matt. 3:16, 17). When the apostle John wrote of this incident, he said, "I saw the Spirit descending from heaven like a dove, and it abode upon him" (John 1:32). It is clear that these persons present at Christ's baptism saw something visible. Luke writes, "And the Holy Ghost descended in a bodily shape like a dove upon him . . ." (Luke 3:22).

What lesson can we learn from this? First, the dove is the emblem of *purity*. Solomon, when speaking to his bride, says, "My dove, my undefiled" (S. of Sol. 5:2). Naturalists tell us that the dove is known for its cleanliness. The dove was acceptable as a sacrifice to the Lord (Lev. 12:6; cf. Luke 2:22-24). When our Lord drove out the moneychangers from the temple, He "overthrew . . . the seats of them that sold doves" (Matt. 21:12; Mark 11:15). The doves were being sold for sacrifices.

The first mention of the dove in Scripture occurs in connection with Noah and the flood. For forty days and nights it rained until the waters had covered the earth. After the waters had abated, Noah sent out from the ark a raven and a dove. The raven found the scene of desolation congenial to its own unclean nature and so it did not return to the ark. But the dove, seeing nothing to attract its pure nature, "found no rest for the sole of her foot, and she returned unto him into the ark" (Gen. 8:6-9). The raven was content to light upon a dead carcass, but such held no attraction for the dove.

The Holy Spirit will not abide in that which is unclean. His coming upon Jesus at His baptism indicated the purity of the Son of God. Paul said that Christ "knew no sin" (2 Cor. 5:21); Peter wrote that He "did no sin" (1 Peter 2:22); and John added, "In him is no sin" (1 John 3:5). When the Holy Spirit in the form of a dove came upon our Lord, it was not to make Him pure, but rather to put the divine seal of approval upon Him "who is holy, harmless, undefiled, separate from sinners" (Heb. 7:26).

When the sinner trusts Christ and is born again, he is made clean, thereby becoming a fit vessel for the Holy Spirit. The body of the child of God is the temple of the Holy Ghost; no unsaved person is indwelt by the Holy Spirit. At the time of the sinner's regeneration we become "partakers of the divine nature" (2 Peter 1:4), but not until then. When Paul asked the Christians at Corinth, "What? know ye not that your body is the temple of the Holy Ghost which is in you, which ye have of God, and ye are not your own?" he added, "For ye are bought with a price" (1 Cor. 6:19, 20). You see, they had already been redeemed, "sanctified in Christ Jesus" (1:2). The Holy Dove abides only in sanctified bodies.

Second, the dove is the emblem of *peace*. There is a proverbial harmlessness for which the dove is known. When our Lord sent out His disciples He said, "Behold, I send you forth as sheep in the midst of wolves: be ye therefore wise as serpents, and harmless as doves" (Matt. 10:16). Spirit-controlled persons are not only people of purity, but of peace also. Peace and purity are closely related, for "there is no peace, saith my God, to the wicked" (Isa. 57:21).

I have been told that the dove has no gall. Now, gall is the symbol of bitterness, a fact conveyed where the word *gall* is used in the Scriptures. Zophar said, "The glittering sword cometh out of his gall" (Job 20:25). I have paraphrased Zophar's statement to read, "All strife emanates from a bitter spirit." Where the Holy Spirit has not come to abide, there cannot be peace. Peter said to Simon the sorcerer, "Repent therefore of this thy wickedness. . . . For I perceive that thou art in the gall of bitterness, and in the bond of iniquity" (Acts 8:22, 23). Simon was not saved, therefore the Holy Spirit was not in him. He was not at peace *with* God nor did he have the peace *of* God. Only bitterness can result when the heart resists the cleansing power of God's Word and the Holy Spirit.

The Holy Dove has no gall, so He produces in the believer His gall-less nature, which is peace and gentleness. Paul wrote, "The kingdom of God is . . . peace . . . in the Holy Ghost" (Rom. 14:17), and "The fruit of the Spirit is . . . peace" (Gal. 5:22). People who are truly saved have peace with God, and they are at peace among themselves. The bitter spirit is in the life of that person who resists and grieves the Holy Spirit. When Israel disobeyed God, the people confessed, "The LORD our God hath put us to silence, and given us water of gall to drink, because we have sinned against the Lord" (Jer. 8:14). Oh, my friends, let us forsake our sins lest that same awful bitterness overtake us.

The Wind

In both the Old and New Testaments the wind is a fitting symbol of the Holy Spirit. One does not need to stretch the imagination to discover the spiritual analogy between the winds of heaven and the Holy Spirit. The New Testament Greek word for "spirit" is *pneuma,* meaning breath, wind, air, spirit. The doctrine of the Holy Spirit is called *pneumatology.*

Man's beginning is described as follows: "And the LORD God formed man of the dust of the ground, and breathed into his nostrils the breath[or spirit] of life; and man became a living soul" (Gen. 2:7). The life imparted to man is the Breath, or Spirit of God. Job said, "All the while my breath is in me, and the spirit of God is in my nostrils" (Job 27:3). The breath that is in man is the divine breathing. Job said also, "The spirit of God hath made me, and the breath of the Almighty hath given me life" (Job 33:4). Isaiah said, "Thus saith God the LORD, he that created the heavens, and stretched them out; he that spread forth the earth, and that which cometh out of it; he that giveth breath unto the people upon it, and spirit to them that walk therein" (Isa. 42:5). Paul, in his sermon at Athens, said, "He giveth to all life, and breath, and all things; . . . For in him we live, and move, and have our being" (Acts 17:25-28). These verses indicate the analogy between the wind (or breath) and the Holy Spirit. The Breath which God breathed into man was the activity of the Holy Spirit.

The spiritual analogy between the Holy Spirit and the wind appears in Ezekiel 37. The vision of the valley of dry bones is not unfamiliar to students of the Bible. The vision was intended to show the spiritual condition of Israel nationally during the long centuries of the Times of the Gentiles, that period during which God would set aside the Jewish nation. This condition of Israel is described by Paul as one of "blindness in part" (Rom. 11:25). It was the vision of blind, lifeless Israel which God showed to the prophet Ezekiel when He set him down in the midst of the valley (Ezek. 37:11). The bones were "very many" and "very dry" (v. 2). God then asked the question, "Son of man, can these bones live?" The prophet answered, "O Lord GOD, thou knowest" (v. 3).

At this point God commanded Ezekiel to prophesy. "O ye dry bones, hear the word of the LORD. Thus saith the Lord GOD unto these bones; Behold, I will cause breath to enter into you, and ye shall live: And I will lay sinews upon you, and will bring up flesh upon you, and cover you with skin, and put breath in you, and ye shall live; and ye shall know that I am the LORD" (vv. 4-6). Obviously there is to be a reconstruction of the bones, and flesh is to cover them again. Ezekiel saw all of this clearly in the vision. The bones represented "the whole house of Israel," the nation that God would yet restore.

But notice next where the emphasis is placed. God said, "I will cause *breath* to enter into you" (v. 5) "and put *breath* in you" (v. 6), because "there was no *breath* in them" (v. 8). Then God said to Ezekiel, "Prophesy unto the *wind*, prophesy, son of man, and say to the *wind*, Thus saith the Lord GOD; Come from the four *winds*, O *breath*, and *breathe* upon these slain, that they may live. So I prophesied as he commanded me, and the *breath* came into them, and they lived, and stood up upon their feet, an exceeding great army" (vv. 9, 10). It is obvious that the words *wind* and *breath* are used synonymously.

Now note the prophesy of the literal fulfillment which is still future for the nation of Israel. God said, "And [I] shall put my *Spirit* in you, and ye shall live, and I shall place you in your own land . . ." (v. 14). Here the Spirit is the Holy Spirit, called the *breath*, or *wind* of God. When God told Ezekiel to speak to the "wind" (v. 9), He meant that the prophet should pray to the *Holy Spirit*, for it is by the power of the Holy Spirit that Israel will be raised and revived spiritually.

On the day of Pentecost "there came a sound from heaven as of a rushing mighty wind, . . . And they were all filled with the Holy Ghost" (Acts 2:2, 4). If those disciples were acquainted with the teachings of the Old Testament, especially

Ezekiel 37, they surely recognized the spiritual analogy between the movement of the wind and the Holy Spirit.

Another illustration of the wind as a figure of the Holy Spirit is in our Lord's teaching of the new birth in His conversation with Nicodemus. Jesus said to him, "Except a man be born again, he cannot see the kingdom of God" (John 3:3). Not grasping the meaning of our Lord's statement, Nicodemus asked, "How can a man be born when he is old? can he enter the second time into his mother's womb, and be born?" (v. 4). To that question our Lord replied, "The *wind* bloweth where it listeth, and thou hearest the sound thereof, but canst not tell whence it cometh, and whither it goeth: so is everyone that is born of the *Spirit*" (v. 8).

I have purposely omitted Christ's words explaining the means of regeneration because they are not particularly relevant to our present study. Yet I have italicized the words *wind* and *Spirit*. While the wind itself is not visible to the human eye, we can hear, see, and feel its effects. There are some things in the scientific realm which are not possible of measurement or explanation, yet we know they exist. Man can neither control nor determine the direction of the winds. Meteorologists admit to a certain enigma about the wind; for this reason your local "weatherman" cannot always predict with accuracy the weather conditions. There is a mystery about the wind. We do know that the winds are air in motion.

There is likewise an unseen and inexplicable movement of the Holy Spirit. The wise preacher said, "Thou knowest not what is the way of the Spirit" (Eccl. 11:5). In some mysterious way He breathes upon the sinner, convicting him of sin (John 16:8) and regenerating him (Titus 3:5). Though His movements are at times mysterious, no one can deny the results of His power in the heart and life of one who yields to Him.

THE FIRE

Moses wrote by divine inspiration, "For the LORD thy God is a consuming *fire*" (Deut. 4:24; cf. Heb. 12:29). He wrote also the following, "And the sight of the glory of the LORD was like devouring *fire* on the top of the mount in the eyes of the children of Israel'' (Exod. 24:17). When Moses recorded God's first appearance to him, he said, "And the angel of the Lord appeared . . . in a flame of *fire* out of the midst of a bush: and he looked, and, behold, the bush burned with *fire*, and the bush was not consumed'' (Exod. 3:2). These passages suffice to introduce the idea that fire is used in the Bible as a symbol of the divine presence. "He is like a refiner's *fire*" (Mal. 3:2).

When the Holy Spirit descended on the day of Pentecost, there was the sign of *sound*, "a rushing mighty wind" (Acts 2:2), and the sign of *sight* when "there appeared unto them cloven tongues like as of fire" (v. 3). And then follows the statement, "And they were all filled with the Holy Ghost" (v. 4). Both the wind and the fire were symbols of the Holy Spirit.

There are practical lessons to be gleaned from the scriptural use of the figure of fire.

Fire gives *light*. Here is suggested the illumination the Holy Spirit provides. He is the Light that illuminates the sacred pages of God's Word, making clear and understandable the deep things of God. "But as it is written, Eye hath not seen, or ear heard, neither have entered into the heart of man, the things which God hath prepared for them that love him. But God hath revealed them unto us by his Spirit: for the Spirit searcheth all things, yea, the deep things of God" (1 Cor. 2:9, 10). The Holy Spirit is the Author of the Holy Scriptures and is therefore the Christian's only reliable teacher of its great truths. He is called "the spirit of wisdom and revelation," that "the eyes of your understanding being enlightened, . . . ye may know" (Eph. 1:17, 18).

Fire gives *warmth*. We know something of the cheerful, warming effects of a glowing fire on a cold, wintry night. The prophet wrote, "I am warm, I have seen the fire" (Isa. 44:16). There is a need today for the warming fire of the Holy Spirit. It has been a long, cold winter spiritually in many churches; the coldness is in pulpit and pew. Our Lord said to the church at Laodicea, "I know thy works, that thou art neither cold nor hot: I would thou wert cold or hot. So then because thou art lukewarm, and neither cold nor hot, I will spue thee out of my mouth. . . . he that hath an ear, let him hear what the Spirit saith unto the churches" (Rev. 3:15, 16, 22). Church life and service need to be set on fire of the Holy Spirit.

Fire *purifies*. Malachi, depicting the coming of Jesus to reign, said, "He shall sit as a refiner and purifier of silver: and shall *purify* the sons of Levi, and purge them as gold and silver" (Mal. 3:3). What Christ will do for Israel in the Millennium, the Holy Spirit is doing in the church today. The body of the Christian is the temple of the Holy Spirit (1 Cor. 3:16; 6:19, 20). As the "Spirit of burning" He purges the dross from our lives, purifying us for worship and service.

In the worship of Israel there was a continual burnt offering. The fire upon the altar was to burn continually; God had said, "It shall never go out" (Lev. 6:12, 13). The Holy Spirit in us desires to consume the dross from our lives and refine the gold. As the silversmith tempers the fire and watches the metal, the action of the flame is revealed. Gradually the dross comes to the surface, and he skims it off, leaving the pure metal. The fire is essential for the purifying process.

We are exhorted to "quench not the Spirit" (1 Thess. 5:19). He wants only to purge the dross from us in order that we should reflect the image of Christ before others. As the silversmith sits before the vat, he continues skimming the dross until he sees his own reflection in the molten metal. Silversmiths have called this reflection "the silver look." Christlikeness is God's goal for every Christian. If we quench the Holy Fire now, our works will not stand up under the test at the Judgment Seat of Christ. "Every man's work shall be made manifest: for the day shall declare it, because it shall be revealed by fire; and the fire shall try every man's work of what sort it is" (1 Cor. 3:13).

The Water

Of all human wants, thirst is perhaps the most exigent of them all. How tormenting when one cannot slake the craving for a refreshing drink of water! Our Lord told of the rich man who died: and in hades being tormented in the flame, he called to Abraham begging him to dip the tip of his finger in water and cool his tongue (Luke 16:22-24). Though our Lord used the language of the physical, I am of the opinion that the thirst of the rich man was spiritual, because it was not his body that was in hades but his spirit. It is spiritual thirst we consider here.

In the heart of every human there is a craving for a certain satisfaction which cannot be found in the springs of this world. God calls and says, "Ho, every one that thirsteth, come ye to the waters . . ." (Isa. 55:1). Here God is represented as standing in the midst of a desert-world, calling to His thirsty throngs to come and drink. One cannot read this passage in Isaiah without giving thought to those words of the Lord Jesus when, on the great day of the Feast of Tabernacles, He stood amid the hurrying crowds and cried, "If any man thirst, let him come unto me and drink. He that believeth on me, as the scripture hath said, out of his belly shall flow rivers of living water." And then the inspired writer adds, "But this spake he of the Spirit . . ." (John 7:37-39). The word *water* here is used symbolically of the Holy Spirit.

In the Old Testament also, water is used as a symbol of the Holy Spirit. God had said, "For I will pour water upon him that is thirsty, and floods upon the dry ground: I will pour my spirit upon thy seed, and my blessing upon thine offspring" (Isa. 44:3). There is a future blessing for Israel to be accomplished by the outpouring of the Holy Spirit who is here likened to water.

Water is *essential to life*. This colorless liquid compound of hydrogen and oxygen (H_2O) is one of the indispensables of man's existence. He cannot survive without it. Water is not a luxury, but a necessity. Even so the Holy Spirit is indispensable to spiritual life. Apart from Him the sinner remains dead in trespasses and sins, and without Him we Christians cannot grow spiritually. We were made "to drink into one Spirit" when we were saved (1 Cor. 12:13), and we need to quench our spiritual thirst now that we are saved. "Blessed are they which do . . . *thirst* after righteousness" (Matt. 5:6). Some

61

people thirst for pleasure, some for wealth, and others for fame. But the cisterns of this world are dry and cannot satisfy. Only the pure water of the Spirit can satisfy the heart of man. Jesus said, "He that believeth on me shall never thirst" (John 6:35).

Water is *essential to growth*. Bildad asked, "Can the flag grow without water?" (Job 8:11). The water-reed flourishes when its roots reach the water, but without the water it withers. In the same way, the Spirit's continuing ministry in the Christian's life is essential to growth. As we "walk in the Spirit" and are "led of the Spirit," we will bear the "fruit of the Spirit" (Gal. 5:16, 18, 22, 23). The blessed man "shall be like a tree planted by the rivers of water, that bringeth forth his fruit in his season" (Ps. 1:3).

Every river cuts its own course by the very force of the flow. The Grand Canyon is evidence that neither mountains nor forests can prevent a river from reaching the sea. "He cutteth out rivers among the rocks; and his eye seeth every precious thing" (Job 28:10). When the Holy Spirit is in control of our lives, there is no obstacle too great to overcome.

Water *produces power*. Niagara Falls is an example of the tremendous unused power that can be harnessed from the world's vast water supply. But the greatest unused power in all the world is the Holy Spirit who dwells in every Christian. I sincerely believe that the average church could continue to function as an organization and pay its bills even if the Holy Spirit did not exist. The early church saw people saved and miracles take place because its ministers and members were filled with the Holy Spirit (Acts 2:4; 4:8, 31; 13:9, 52). Paul said, "My speech and my preaching was not with enticing words of man's wisdom, but in demonstration of the Spirit and of power" (1 Cor. 2:4).

We use power in our worship, power in our preaching, power in our witnessing, power in all our service, but it must be the Holy Spirit's power and not ours. You see, water is God's gift to man. With all of man's scientific progress, he is not able to create water. Water is not a product of the earth; it comes first from heaven. Even so does spiritual power come from God the Holy Spirit. We spend ourselves in the energy of the flesh and produce nothing. But when the Holy Spirit is in control of our lives, His power operates in and through us.

God said to His people, "Thou shalt be like a watered garden, and like a spring of water, whose waters fail not" (Isa. 58:11). No matter how difficult and evil the times in which we live might be, the child of God can be a channel of blessing to others. Jesus said, "But ye shall receive power, after that the Holy Ghost is come upon you: and ye shall be witnesses unto me both in Jerusalem, and in all Judea, and in Samaria, and unto the uttermost part of the earth" (Acts 1:8).

THE OIL

Oil in the Bible is an impressive symbol of the Holy Spirit. When Aaron was made high priest, he was anointed with oil. God said, "Thou shalt take the anointing oil, and pour it upon his head, and anoint him" (Exod. 29:7). When Samuel anointed Saul with oil to become Israel's first king, we read, "The spirit of God came upon him" (1 Sam. 10:1, 10). Likewise, when Samuel took the horn of oil and anointed David, "The spirit of the LORD came upon David from that day forward" (1 Sam. 16:13). The anointing with oil was symbolic of the anointing of the Holy Spirit for a special service.

The apostle Peter, in the house of Cornelius, said, "God anointed Jesus of Nazareth with the Holy Ghost and with power" (Acts 10:38). Peter was possibly referring to the time when the Holy Spirit descended in a bodily shape like a dove upon Him (Luke 3:22). Jesus Himself said, "The Spirit of the Lord is upon me, because he hath anointed me . . ." (Luke 4:18). This incident in Christ's life was doubtless the fulfillment of those predictions in Psalm 45:7 and Isaiah 61:1, referring to the Spirit's anointing Him just prior to His public ministry.

Oil, with fire, *supplies illumination*. In the tabernacle in the wilderness there were three lights: (1) the natural light in the court; (2) the candlestick (or lampstand) in the Holy

63

Place; (3) the glory of God in the Holy of Holies. The lampstand in the Holy Place was the most beautiful and most ornamental piece of furniture in the tabernacle. However, it was not placed there as an ornament, but to give light in an otherwise dark place. It was made of pure gold, Christ Himself being represented in the main shaft and having the preeminence, and His followers represented by the branches. Now the branches were not the light in themselves, but merely the receptacles for the light. There could be no light except when the branches remained united to the main shaft and the bowls were kept filled with oil (Exod. 25:31-40; 37:17-24).

An application to the above seems clear. The six branches from the main shaft of the candelabra in the tabernacle represent the believers in Christ. Six is man's number. God created him on the sixth day. The number of the Antichrist is 666, representing the sum total of human wisdom and power.

But the Christian is to show forth the true light. Jesus said, "I am the light of the world" (John 8:12), "the true light, which lighteth every man that cometh into the world" (John 1:9). Later Jesus added, "As long as I am in the world, I am the light of the world" (John 9:5), and "yet a little while is the light with you" (John 12:35). Christ knew His earthly mission would be brief, so He gathered around Him His own followers and said to them, "Ye are the light of the world" (Matt. 5:14). He assured them that after He left them to return to His Father, He would send the Spirit, the Holy Oil, to keep the Light shining. Yes, we Christians are the light of the world indwelt by the Holy Spirit. Just as the lampstand in the tabernacle could give forth light only as it was kept filled with oil, even so must we be filled with the Spirit.

The prevailing spiritual and moral darkness about us is sufficient evidence that there is need for the Light. What a dark place this world is! And if we are to maintain a spiritual glow we will have to keep our wicks trimmed of pride, prejudice, jealousy, and selfishness so that we might show forth the person of our Lord Jesus Christ.

The Lord said of John the Baptist, "He was a burning and a

shining light'' (John 5:35). Why was this true of John? Before John's birth, God sent an angel to his father with this message: ''For he [John] shall be great in the sight of the Lord, and shall drink neither wine nor strong drink; and he shall be filled with the Holy Ghost, even from his mother's womb'' (Luke 1:15). John was Spirit-controlled, thus he was an illuminator, glowing brightly during the brief period he was here on earth. John bore a faithful witness to Jesus Christ (John 1:29), and Jesus bore a mighty witness to John (Luke 7:28). John did not hide his light under a bushel.

Jesus said, ''Ye are the light of the world. A city that is set on a hill cannot be hid. Neither do men light a candle, and put it under a bushel, but on a candlestick; and it giveth light unto all that are in the house. Let your light so shine before men, that they may see your good works, and glorify your Father which is in heaven'' (Matt. 5:14-16). John obeyed the Lord's admonition. And this we must do. Paul wrote, ''That ye may be blameless and harmless, the sons of God, without rebuke, in the midst of a crooked and perverse nation, among whom ye shine as lights in the world'' (Phil. 2:15). One look at conditions in the world and we must conclude that the shadows are lengthening and the midnight hour is close at hand. ''Let us therefore cast off the works of darkness, and let us put on the armour of light'' (Rom. 13:12).

In the use of oil as a symbol of the Holy Spirit, there is a solemn warning to the unsaved. I recall our Lord's parable of the ten virgins (Matt. 25:1-13). This parable has in it a message to all who are religious, but who have not been born again of the Holy Spirit.

The ten virgins represent those who, by their religious profession, stand in a place of testimony. Five of them were wise, having taken oil in their vessels with their lamps; but the other five were unwise, having taken their lamps but no oil. All ten professedly went forth to meet the bridegroom. While they waited for His coming they all slept. Then at midnight a cry was heard, ''Behold, the bridegroom cometh; go ye out to meet him.''

The five who took oil were wise unto salvation because

65

they had been born of the Spirit. They were ready to meet the Bridegroom. The five unwise had no oil and therefore were left behind; though they knocked and sought diligently to be admitted, they were shut out forever. The Lord said to them, "I know ye not."

THE FINGER

We conclude this chapter with a brief study of the expression, "the Finger of God." This term is a biblical one which the Lord Jesus used. The Pharisees had accused Christ of casting out demons by the power of Beelzebub, the prince of demons. Matthew records our Lord as having said, "I cast out demons by the *Spirit* of God" (Matt. 12:28). Luke's account reads, "I with the *finger* of God cast out demons" (Luke 11:20). There is no contradiction here. The two expressions "the Spirit of God" and "the finger of God" are used synonymously.

First, we see the Finger of God (the Holy Spirit) in inspiration. Two references in the Old Testament to the Finger of God speak of the giving of God's Word to man. "And he gave unto Moses, when he had made an end of communing with him upon Mount Sinai, two tables of testimony, tables of stone, written with the finger of God" (Exod. 31:18). Later Moses testified, "And the Lord delivered unto me two tables of stone written with the finger of God . . ." (Deut. 9:10).

Now we know that the expression "the Finger of God" is a symbolical term, inasmuch as God does not have fingers. "God is a Spirit" (John 4:24), and Jesus said that a spirit does not have flesh and bones (Luke 24:39). Human fingers penned the manuscripts of Holy Scripture, but they were controlled by the Holy Spirit. "Holy men of God spake as they were moved by the Holy Ghost" (2 Peter 1:21). "All scripture is given by inspiration of God" (2 Tim. 3:16). The Bible is the product of the Holy Spirit. This is the Finger of God in inspiration.

Next, we see the Finger of God (the Holy Spirit) demonstrating divine sovereignty over evil spirits. We find it in

66

Luke's account of our Lord's casting out demons, recorded in Luke 11:14-26. The Lord Jesus had cast out a demon from one who had been stricken speechless, and the dumb person began to speak (v. 14). Christ's enemies did not deny that a miracle had been performed but, so that they might discredit Him in the eyes of the astonished onlookers, they accused Him of being in league with the devil. They said, "He casteth out devils through Beelzebub the chief of the devils" (v. 15). In substance they were saying that Jesus was able to cast out demons only because He was in alliance with Satan, the prince of the demons. They knew that demons are subject to a leader.

But our Lord knew their thoughts and evil intentions. He answered them, "Every kingdom divided against itself is brought to desolation; and a house divided against itself falleth. If Satan also be divided against himself, how shall his kingdom stand?" (vv. 17, 18). How absurd was their accusation! Actually *they* were in league with the devil. Their crowd had effected cures, but not by the power of God (v. 19).

Christ represented the kingdom of God, not the kingdom of darkness. His miracles were performed by the power of the Holy Spirit, "the Finger of God" (v. 20). Early in His ministry Jesus said, "The Spirit of the Lord is upon me" (Luke 4:18). Peter testified to "how God anointed Jesus of Nazareth with the Holy Ghost and with power: Who went about doing good, and healing all that were oppressed of the devil; for God was with him" (Acts 10:38). He demonstrated how satanic power and worldly opposition are no match for the Finger of God.

Another reference to the Finger of God in the Old Testament is associated with the revelation of the judgment of God recorded in Daniel 5. Belshazzar made a feast for a thousand of his lords. During the banquet, drunkenness and base sensuality prevailed. Made drunk by the alcoholic beverage he consumed, Belshazzar sent for the sacred vessels of Jehovah and made a royal joke of them.

Suddenly, out of the sleeve of that night of debauchery, there appeared fingers which wrote across the wall of the banquet hall the words, MENE, MENE, TEKEL, UPHARSIN. The Holy Spirit, whom Belshazzar had resisted, had spelled out the wicked king's doom. The king was weighed in God's scales and found wanting. Now the end of his kingdom had come; already the Medes and the Persians were at the gates (Dan. 5:5-28). The same Spirit who spoke to him through the sacred writings now ceased to strive with him. Belshazzar's day of reckoning had come.

Centuries before Belshazzar's death, another Gentile ruler defied God. Pharaoh refused to let Israel go, and God sent devastating plagues upon Egypt until Pharaoh cried, "This is the finger of God" (Exod. 8:19). He too learned that when a person resists the Hoy Spirit's conviction, he cannot escape the Spirit's condemnation.

These figures of the Holy Spirit do not form the foundation of creed or doctrine. They were included in the Word of God that we might know that the Holy Spirit is in the world, and that we might know Him better who is able to guide us into all truth.

Study Questions

1. How does the dove symbolize the Holy Spirit?
2. Why is the wind an appropriate symbol for the Holy Spirit?
3. How does fire symbolize the Holy Spirit?
4. In what ways does water symbolize the Holy Spirit?
5. How does oil symbolize the Holy Spirit?
6. What is the work of the Spirit as "the Finger of God"?

Chapter 6

The Filling With the Holy Spirit

Of the several aspects of the person and work of the Holy Spirit, none is more vital to the Christian's growth and spirituality than the filling of the Spirit. The Spirit's filling is the means by which He controls the behavior and performs His ministries through the believer.

The Word of God divides believers into two classifications, those who are "carnal" and those who are "spiritual" (1 Cor. 3:1). The carnal Christian is a person controlled by the flesh; he lives according to the dictates and power of his own selfish desires. The spiritual Christian is the person controlled by the Holy Spirit; he lives according to the dictates and power of the Spirit.

Carnality and spirituality are opposites. "This I say then, Walk in the Spirit, and ye shall not fulfil the lust of the flesh. For the flesh lusteth against the Spirit, and the Spirit against the flesh: and these are contrary the one to the other: so that ye cannot do the things that ye would" (Gal. 5:16, 17). Paul states simply that there is a conflict between the two natures in the Christian. He admitted to this conflict within himself when he wrote his Epistle to the Romans (Rom. 7:14-23).

Every Christian experiences this inner struggle. The sincere child of God has the desire to do the will of God at all times, but his big problem is doing it. I desire that in this present study we might see those truths in the Bible that will guide us toward adjusting to God's plan and His process for spiritual growth.

Here I sound a note of caution. Beware of the modern trend in some religious circles which teaches a quick, easy way to instant spirituality. Be assured that there is no shortcut to the Spirit-filled life. Many years ago I read the book *Holiness: the False and the True,* by the late Dr. H. A. Ironside; this little volume guided me in my early Christian experience. In it Dr. Ironside wrote, "Nowhere in Scripture is it taught that there is a sudden leap to be taken from carnality to spirituality, or from a life of comparative unconcern as to godliness to one of intense devotion to Christ. On the contrary, increase in piety is ever presented as a growth, which should be as normal and natural as the orderly progression in human life from infancy to full stature." Dr. Ironside is in agreement with Scripture. He knew the meaning of the Spirit-filled life.

Miles Stanford warns the believer to beware of the kind of workshop in which you are told to "do your thing." These weekend gatherings often substitute philosophy, psychology, and sociology for Bible doctrine. One leader invited the participants to "do your own thing, express your hostilities, love, scream, laugh, cry, swear, touch, and hug and kiss if necessary." Such behavior as witnessed in some of the "confess and share" groups can only leave the participants in a state of spiritual defeat and ultimate disaster. The "no doctrine" approach cannot possibly lead to the Spirit-controlled life. There are spirits in control, to be sure, but the Holy Spirit is not one of them. "Beloved, believe not every spirit, but try the spirits whether they are of God: because many false prophets are gone out into the world" (1 John 4:1).

THE COMMAND TO BE FILLED

The Spirit-filled life is commanded by God. The apostle Paul wrote, "And be not drunk with wine, wherein is excess;

70

but be filled with the Spirit'' (Eph. 5:18). It is clear that we Christians are expected to be filled with the Spirit. The Spirit-filled life is not optional; it is obligatory.

A. *The Meaning of Being Filled*

A distinction must be made between positional truth and practical teaching. The fact of the believer's position in Christ — which includes his identification with Christ in His death, burial, resurrection, and ascension — is important. We will come to this later in our study when we consider the *conditions* for being filled with the Spirit. However, we must not confuse the matter of the positional with the practical when considering the *command* to be filled.

Certain phases of the Holy Spirit's work are accomplished at the time of the believer's salvation experience. The Holy Spirit is the Father's gift to every believer at the moment of salvation. We are never commanded to be indwelt, sealed, or baptized with the Holy Spirit. Every saved person is indwelt (Rom. 8:9; 1 Cor. 3:16; 6:19), sealed (2 Cor. 1:22; Eph. 1:13; 4:30), and baptized (1 Cor. 12:13). These experiences need not be sought by any child of God. Hearing and believing God's Word and receiving Jesus Christ are all that one needs in order to be indwelt, sealed, and baptized with the Spirit. These ministries of the Spirit are linked with our position in Christ. That is what God did for us the moment we believed.

But we are commanded to be filled with the Spirit. The verb *be filled* in the original text of Ephesians 5:18 is in the present tense, meaning continuous action. It can be translated ''keep being filled.'' Christians are exhorted to have the fullness of the Spirit, to pursue it at all times.

In the early days of the church, believers were filled with the Holy Spirit at Pentecost (Acts 2:4). Later those same Christians experienced another filling (Acts 4:31). Paul was filled with the Spirit shortly after his conversion (Acts 9:17); years later he was filled with the Spirit again (Acts 13:9). Here we learn that the filling of the Spirit is a repeated experience. This was never the case with the Spirit's ministries of indwelling, sealing, or baptism, for these occur once

71

only in every believer, never needing to be repeated. It is a sad reflection on the spiritual state of many Christians that they are regenerated, indwelt, sealed, and baptized, but not filled with the Holy Spirit.

What is meant by being "filled with the Spirit"? The clue to the correct understanding of being filled with the Spirit is in the text where the command is given. "And be not drunk with wine, wherein is excess; but be filled with the Spirit." There is both contrast and comparison between drunkenness and being filled with the Spirit. The analogy appears not less than three times in the New Testament (Luke 1:15; Acts 2:4, 13; Eph. 5:18).

The comparison between drunkenness and being filled with the Spirit is in the matter of *control*. A drunk person is under the control of alcohol, and will think, speak, and act in ways not natural when sober. A Christian who is filled with the Spirit will think, speak, and act in ways not natural when he or she is controlled by the flesh. Thus a Spirit-filled life is simply a Spirit-controlled life.

Our English word *filled* is the translation of several different words in the original text. However, the idea of being controlled seems to dominate.

When our Lord performed His miracle of healing the man with palsy, we read, "And they were all amazed, and they glorified God, and were filled with fear, saying, We have seen strange things today" (Luke 5:26). The sight of paralytics was a common one, but what was uncommon was the instantaneous cure of a paralytic. At the sight of the miracle they were controlled by fear.

A little later, Christ entered a synagogue and there saw a man whose right hand was withered. At Jesus' command, the man stretched forth his hand, and immediately the hand was completely healed. Because it was the Sabbath Day, Christ's enemies took advantage of the occasion to attack Him. Luke says, "And they were filled with madness; and communed one with another what they might do to Jesus" (Luke 6:6-11). In that instance madness controlled Christ's enemies.

When Christ told His disciples that He was going to leave

them, and that they would be persecuted after His departure, He observed their reaction. He said, "Because I have said these things unto you, sorrow hath filled your heart" (John 16:6). They were suddenly controlled, dominated by sorrow.

In the early days of the church, Ananias sold some property and brought part of the money to the disciples to be used in the Lord's work. Ananias pretended that he brought the full price from the sale of his field. Peter, having the gift of "discerning of spirits" (1 Cor. 12:10), said, "Ananias, why hath Satan filled thine heart to lie to the Holy Ghost, and to keep back part of the price of the land?" (Acts 5:1-4). Ananias, being controlled by Satan, was led to lie and deceive.

When the Father sent the Holy Spirit to dwell in us, it was that He might fill or control us. The Christian who is filled with the Spirit is not merely indwelt by the Spirit, but also controlled by the Spirit.

B. *The Misunderstanding About Being Filled*

Do not confuse the filling with the baptism. Some of God's choice servants have fallen into this error, among them the late Dr. R. A. Torrey. By his careless use of the words *baptism* and *filling,* Dr. Torrey created much confusion. He insisted upon referring to the *filling* as "the baptism of the Spirit"; he taught that "the baptism with the Holy Spirit is an operation distinct from and subsequent and additional to His regenerating work." To this day there are followers of the charismatic movement, which I believe is in reality a cult, who quote Dr. Torrey in support of their erroneous teaching. He has been quoted frequently by Pentecostals who found in Torrey's teaching an affinity with their own. To teach, as Torrey did, that a person could or could not be baptized with the Spirit at the moment of regeneration is a serious error.

Nowhere in Scripture is the baptizing work of the Spirit found in past dispensations. It is limited to this present age. It is never mentioned as having been experienced by Old Testament believers or during the time of Christ's ministry on earth. After His resurrection and just before His ascension He said, "Ye shall be baptized with the Holy Ghost not many days hence" (Acts 1:5). It is clear from this passage that the baptizing work of the Holy Spirit was yet future when our Lord made His declaration. This phase of the Spirit's ministry began on the day of Pentecost even as Peter testified that it did (Acts 11:15-17).

That baptism with the Spirit is the universal experience of all believers in this present age. This is proved by the plain teaching of Scripture. The apostle Paul wrote, "For by one Spirit are we all baptized into one body, whether we be Jews or Gentiles, whether we be bond or free; and have been all made to drink into one Spirit" (1 Cor. 12:13). The Christians in the church of Corinth were not spiritual persons, but carnal (3:1); yet they were in the "body." The word *body* is a figure of speech which is used synonymously with the word *church*. "The Church . . . is his [Christ's] body" (Eph. 1:22, 23). The baptizing work of the Spirit is that phase of His ministry which incorporates the believing sinner, at the moment he is saved, as a living member into the body of Christ. Apart from the baptizing work of the Holy Spirit there is no way that a person can be joined to Jesus Christ and His church.

If the baptism were not experienced by all Christians, one should expect to find some place in the New Testament epistles a command or an exhortation to be baptized. But no such command or exhortation appears. Moreover, there is no scriptural reference which would so much as hint that a saved person was ever baptized by the Spirit a second time. There is only "one baptism" (Eph. 4:5).

I will not say that there is never an experience emanating from Spirit-baptism: there are numerous experiences in the Christian's life resultant of being baptized into the body of Christ. However, every child of God should know that the baptizing work of the Holy Spirit is in itself nonexperiential. This truth will help prevent any believer from associating an experience, such as speaking in tongues, with Spirit-baptism. I have met and known persons, whom I believe were truly born again, who were totally unaware of the

74

biblical truth that they had been baptized into the body of Christ.

Actually there are two results of the baptism of the Holy Spirit. First, the baptizing effects our union with Christ. Not less than seventy times in the Epistles the believer is said to be "in Christ." The child of God, having been baptized by the Spirit, is joined to Christ. This is a new union which is unknown to the unsaved. Any person can join a denomination or an organized church without being joined to Jesus Christ, but at the time of salvation, the baptizing work with the Spirit actualizes the vital union with Christ. "Know ye not that your bodies are the members of Christ?" (1 Cor. 6:15). "For as many of you as have been baptized into Christ have put on Christ" (Gal. 3:27).

There is a unique oneness that exists between Jesus Christ and the believer, comparable to the oneness between the Father and the Son. Jesus said to His disciples, "At that day ye shall know that I am in my Father, and ye in me, and I in you" (John 14:20). That blessed union between Christ and the believer was accomplished by the baptizing work of the Holy Spirit, and it can never be broken.

Second, the baptizing work of the Holy Spirit effects the union of all believers with each other. "Now ye are the body of Christ, and members in particular" (1 Cor. 12:27). "So we, being many, are one body in Christ, and every one members one of another" (Rom. 12:5). "For ye are all the children of God by faith in Christ Jesus. . . . There is neither Jew nor Greek, there is neither bond nor free, there is neither male nor female: for ye are all one in Christ Jesus" (Gal. 3:26, 28). We Christians had no part in effecting this wonderful union. It was accomplished through the baptizing work of the Holy Spirit (1 Cor. 12:13). Nor can that union ever be broken. However, we are exhorted to be at peace with every other member of the body, "endeavouring to keep the unity of the Spirit in the bond of peace" (Eph. 4:3). "That there should be no schism in the body; but that the members should have the same care one for another" (1 Cor. 12:25).

Make certain, then, that you do not confuse the *baptism*

with the *filling*. The terms are not synonymous, nor are they ever used interchangeably in Scripture. The baptism with the Holy Spirit is that once-for-all transaction whereby believing sinners are brought into the true church and thus united to Christ and to each other.

THE CONDITIONS FOR BEING FILLED

Not all Christians live on the same spiritual level. There is an obvious difference in the behavior of Christians. We know this both from the teaching of Scripture and from personal experience. There are "carnal" Christians and "spiritual" Christians (1 Cor. 3:1). There are Christians who "grow up," and there are those who don't (Eph. 4:15; 1 Peter 2:2; 2 Peter 3:18). In the language of the apostle John there are three levels of growth in God's family: "little children . . . young men . . . fathers" (1 John 2:12, 13). The Epistle to the Hebrews speaks of the "babe" and "them that are of full age" (Heb. 5:13, 14). There are those who walk after the manner of men (1 Cor. 3:3), and those who "walk worthy of the Lord" (Col. 1:10). Thus the language of Scripture acknowledges a difference in the quality of the day-by-day life of Christians.

Being filled with the Spirit is indispensable to growth and spirituality. As a young pastor I struggled with a bad situation — namely, my ministry lacked power. Then one day I heard L. L. Legters teaching on the Spirit-filled life, at a summer Bible Conference in Keswick, New Jersey. I returned home from that meeting determined to investigate the subject more thoroughly. What I heard from Dr. Legters, and the additional truth I gleaned in my study, convinced me of the sad fact that I was a preacher who was not filled with the Spirit.

I had graduated from a well-known school of the Bible, so I had truth, but it was truth divorced from power. I had the "form of godliness" but not the power (2 Tim. 3:5). I was guilty of what the late Dr. Ironside called "trafficking in unfelt truth." We cannot by-pass the plain fact that the results of the Pentecostal sermon were due largely to the experience of the disciples, namely, "They were all filled with the Holy

76

Ghost." The filling with the Holy Spirit is indispensable to effective service for Jesus Christ.

Are there certain conditions for being filled? If so, what are they, and how can they be met? Yes, there are conditions, prerequisite to being filled with the Spirit. Let us examine them.

A. *A Fact to Be Acknowledged*

A victorious Christian experience bears unfailing testimony to the fact that sin has been dealt with. But mark well, not merely the *symptoms* have been dealt with, but the *source*. Therefore the Christian must take into account his identification with Christ in His death, his co-crucifixion with Christ. Romans 6 states the matter clearly.

> We . . . are dead to sin (6:2).
> Knowing this, that our old man is crucified with him, that the body of sin might be destroyed, that henceforth we should not serve sin (6:6).
> For he that is dead is freed from sin (6:7).
> Likewise reckon ye also yourselves to be dead indeed unto sin (6:11),
> For sin shall not have dominion over you (6:14).

That is a fact we must acknowledge.

Yes, we are back at the Cross, and rightly so. If we by-pass the judicial judgment of Christ's death upon the old nature, and the application of our positional crucifixion with Christ, we are left to struggle with the problem of sin. I do not suggest that we Christians need not confess our sins in order to be filled with the Spirit. Indeed we must! But after I have confessed a known sin, I have dealt only with the symptom, passing over Christ's provision for freedom from the guilt and penalty of sin. The Cross effected the judicial judgment of sin upon the old nature.

The ministry of Dr. Legters helped me to see the much-needed truth — namely, the self-life is the source of sin, and the Cross is God's remedy for the sin nature. When Christ died, I died. In His own miraculous way — deeply mysterious, yet nevertheless true — God put my sinful nature to death on the Cross with the Lord Jesus Christ. In no way can the sin nature produce anything that is good. God knew this, so He passed the sentence of death upon it, nailing it to the Cross. Most Christians know that Christ died for their *sins*, but too few know that He died for the *sin nature* also.

Brothers and sisters in Christ, God has finished with our old nature. Acknowledge this fact and reckon on it. "Reckon ye also yourselves to be dead indeed unto sin" (Rom. 6:11). Paul did. He testified, "I am crucified with Christ" (Gal. 2:20). Since God declared it to be so, why hassle over it? It is beyond the grasp of my finite mind, nevertheless I acknowledge it to be so. The important question is, What is *your* response to the fact of your identification with Christ in His death? Don't miss this! It is the one scriptural truth which helps us to cease from self-effort. This sovereign position becomes to every child of God the source of life and power for victory.

B. *Fallacies to Be Avoided*

Certain fallacies should be avoided in the light of the truth of our identification with Christ.

First, we should avoid the fallacious doctrine of eradication. Those who believe and teach this doctrine tell us that the sin nature can be removed totally or eradicated from the believer. They suggest that after the sin nature has been eliminated, one may come to the experience in which he no longer has a conflict with the sin nature. There have been times when I wished this were true, but such wishing showed up my weakness. Actually at that particular moment I was not wearing the armor God had provided for me, and so I was attempting to avoid the battle completely. The eradication doctrine is not taught in the Bible. It offers no solution to the problem of the sin nature.

Second, we should avoid the fallacy of the self-crucifixion theory. Those who teach this exhort Christians to crucify themselves. "Put yourself to death and you will no longer have a problem with the sin nature," they tell us. I once shared a Bible conference platform with a brother who taught this. We discussed it till long after midnight. He could not see that the secret was in the fact that he had already been identified with Christ in His death. "How many times can you die?" I asked him. I truly pity those deluded persons who struggle to put themselves to death, trying to do something that is humanly impossible. The apostle Paul said, "I am [I have been] crucified with Christ" (Gal. 2:20).

Third, we should avoid grieving the Spirit. This expression occurs once in the New Testament. Paul wrote, "And grieve not the holy Spirit of God, whereby ye are sealed unto the day of redemption" (Eph. 4:30). All believers have the potentiality to grieve the Holy Spirit, and all should know the seriousness of the consequence when we do grieve Him.

The Greek verb translated "grieve" is *lupeō*. It means to cause pain or grief or sorrow. J. Oswald Sanders says, *"Grieve* is a love word. One can anger an enemy, but not grieve him. Only one who loves can be grieved, and the deeper the love the greater the grief."

There are no doubt many sins which grieve the Holy Spirit. But upon examining the context in which the command is given, the sins of speech stand out specifically. Now, the list is not complete. But "lying" and "corrupt communication" and "evil speaking" are mentioned. "Wherefore putting away lying, speak every man truth with his neighbour: for we are members one of another" (Eph. 4:25). "Let no corrupt communication proceed out of your mouth . . ." (4:29). "Let all . . . evil speaking be put away from you . . ." (4:31). These verses make clear that the sins of speech are those which particularly grieve the Holy Spirit. When we are grieving the Holy Spirit, He is not in control. The Christian who would be Spirit-filled must beware of the unguarded tongue.

Fourth, we should avoid quenching the Spirit. "Quench not the Spirit" (1 Thess. 5:19). The verb *quench* (Gr. *sbennumi*) is used metaphorically, referring to both the Holy Spirit and Satan. Paul wrote to the Ephesians, "Put on the whole armour of God, that ye may be able to stand against the wiles of the devil. . . . Above all, taking the shield of faith, wherewith ye shall be able to quench the fiery darts of the wicked" (Eph. 6:11, 16). We quench Satan by hindering his operations. Even so does the believer quench the Holy Spirit by hindering His operations.

But how can we Christians quench the Spirit? Is He not sovereign deity? Is He not all-powerful? Yes, He is both sovereign God and omnipotent; nevertheless He can be quenched, else why the exhortation "quench not the Spirit"?

Out of my personal experience I say to you what I sincerely believe is the major cause of quenching the Spirit. Summed up in one word, it is "self." And if you ask me what self is, I can only reply that it is the "flesh," the big "I." Oh, the subtleties of the self-life! How difficult it is to see ourselves as we really are! A sincere and honest Christian once said, "For I know that in me (that is, in my flesh [self],) dwelleth no good thing" (Rom. 7:18).

It is when the impulses of the flesh usurp the place of the power of the Holy Spirit that we quench Him. The old nature is Satan's busiest workshop, where he operates twenty-four hours of every day. Even after we Christians have overcome the moral evils of our pre-conversion days, the ugly self-life continues to function. We have terminated many evil practices, but have not terminated the self-life. We still tend to want to do as we will. We are guilty of self-will, self-seeking, self-assertion, self-indulgence, self-pity, self-love, self-exaltation, self-justification, and self-confidence.

When we, by an act of the will, dethrone self and enthrone Christ, the Holy Spirit will control us. The flesh and the spirit are in opposition to one another. The desires of one are set against the desires of the other. They are in conflict. When self gives way to Christ, the Holy Spirit is not quenched, and a barrier has been removed for the Christian to be filled with the Spirit.

The Spirit-filled life is a selfless life. It is Christ-centered. Jesus said, "I seek not mine own will" (John 5:30). "And I seek not mine own glory" (John 8:50). "I am meek and lowly in heart" (Matt. 11:29). Are we so different from Christ that His likeness is not seen in us?

Have you ever heard of the "me-bird"? It gets its name from the fact that it has only one sound, "Me-me, Me-me." Don't be a "me-bird," but be able to say with Paul, "Not I, but Christ." Don't quench the Spirit by permitting the flesh to assert itself. Meet the conditions, and you can be filled with the Spirit.

Fifth, avoid the mistake of refusing to desire and seek for the fullness of the Spirit. Jesus said, "If any man thirst, let him come unto me, and drink. . . . He that believeth on me, . . . out of his belly shall flow rivers of living water. . . . This spake he of the Spirit, which they that believe on him should receive . . ." (John 7:37-39). I see in these verses three stages in the Spirit's ministry, His *incoming,* His *infilling,* and His *outflowing*.

Jesus said, "If any man thirst." I meet Christians who have no spiritual thirst; during the first years of my own life as a Christian I had no spiritual thirst. Too many Christians fail to see that being born again and receiving the Holy Spirit is but the first step in the Christian life. A thirsty person wants to quench that thirst. It is not likely that we will know the experience of the Spirit-filled life if we do not desire it. Jesus said, "Blessed are they which do hunger and thirst after righteousness: for they shall be filled" (Matt. 5:6). And I must add that the desire to be filled must have the glory of God as its goal (1 Cor. 10:31). Even the desire to be filled with the Spirit could have behind it an unsanctified ambition.

THE CONSEQUENCES OF BEING FILLED

Let us look again at our text: "And be not drunk with wine, wherein is excess; but be filled with the Spirit" (Eph. 5:18). An interesting observation here is that the Greek word *plerousthe* ("filled") is in the imperative mood. It is a command, a mandate. Further, this verb is in the present tense, expressing continuous action and meaning that the experience is repeated again and again. Finally, the verb *plerousthe* is in the passive voice, which means that the subject is acted upon. Here a person is being acted upon, controlled by a power outside himself.

In this instance the Christian is being acted upon by the Holy Spirit. His thoughts, words, and actions are under the domination of the Spirit. He is a completely changed person, attempting and accomplishing things he never thought of doing. Following are a few of the results or consequences of a Spirit-filled life. Remember that the Spirit-filled life is for all Christians, ordinary Christians in the everyday routine of life, both men and women. The results are extremely practical.

We must take another look at the context in which our text appears. After the command is given to be filled with the Spirit, there follows immediately some consequences, all of which are impossible in the flesh unaided by the Holy Spirit.

First, the Spirit-filled Christian will adore and worship God with a glad heart. "Speaking to yourselves [literally, to one another] in psalms and hymns and spiritual songs, singing and making melody in your heart to the Lord" (Eph. 5:19). True worship is no mere external ritual performed in public houses of worship. Rather it is that warm-hearted praise and thanksgiving that comes only from the heart controlled by the Holy Spirit. Jesus said, "God is a Spirit: and they that worship him must worship him in spirit and in truth" (John 4:24). Such worship is produced in the heart by the Holy Spirit. Even in times of sorrow or suffering the child of God, filled with the Holy Spirit, will praise Him. Such is the natural expression of being controlled by the Spirit.

Second, the Spirit-filled Christian will be thankful at all times and under all conditions. "Giving thanks always for all things unto God and the Father in the name of our Lord Jesus Christ" (Eph. 5:20). Paul wrote to the Colossians, "And whatsoever ye do in word or deed, do all in the name of the Lord Jesus, giving thanks to God and the Father by him" (Col. 3:17). In one of his earliest epistles, the same apostle exhorted the believers, "In everything give thanks: for this is the will of God in Christ Jesus concerning you" (1 Thess. 5:18).

Once when I finished expounding this verse in a Bible conference, a woman spoke to me about it at the close of the meeting. She said, "I don't see how it is humanly possible to give thanks in everything." She was correct. It is not humanly possible — it is possible only in the heart that is filled with the Holy Spirit.

Third, the Spirit-filled Christian is a submissive person. "Submitting yourselves one to another in the fear of God" (Eph. 5:21). Note the punctuation in verses 18-21: the passage is one continuous sentence, all verses being linked to the command to be filled with the Spirit. Spirit-controlled submission cements the marriage relationship and maintains harmony between husbands and wives. "Wives, submit yourselves unto your own husbands, as unto the Lord. . . . Husbands, love your wives, even as Christ also loved the church, and gave himself for it" (Eph. 5:22, 25). When the flesh is in control, self-expression dominates and the harmony is disrupted. When Christians are Spirit filled, there is mutual submission, never self-assertion.

This teaching of the New Testament is peculiar in the light of modern trends. But it is both reasonable and possible. The Spirit-filled wife will respect her husband and accept the role assigned to her by God. Likewise the Spirit-filled husband will show the same kind of love to his wife that Christ showed to us sinners when He died to save us. If Christian husbands and wives were filled with the Spirit, there would be no broken marriages and no divorces.

Fourth, the Spirit-filled Christian is empowered for service and witnessing. Jesus said, "But ye shall receive power, after that the Holy Ghost is come upon you: and ye shall be witnesses unto me both in Jerusalem, and in all Judea, and in Samaria, and unto the uttermost part of the earth" (Acts 1:8). On the day of Pentecost the Spirit came, "and they were all filled with the Holy Ghost" (Acts 2:4). The results of the Pentecostal sermon could not have been produced through human effort apart from the Spirit's power, and that power flowed through those Spirit-filled disciples.

Peter and John were put into prison for healing the impotent man and preaching the Christian message. The following day they were brought before the Council to make a defense.

Here was a new experience for Peter: it was actually an emergency. There was no way that either of the two disciples could have gotten out from that situation.

"Then Peter, *filled with the Holy Ghost,* said unto them, Ye rulers of the people, and elders of Israel, If we this day be examined of the good deed done to the impotent man, by what means he is made whole; Be it known unto you all, and to all the people of Israel, that by the name of Jesus Christ of Nazareth, whom ye crucified, whom God raised from the dead, even by him doth this man stand here before you whole. . . . Now when they saw the boldness of Peter and John, . . . they let them go" (Acts 4:8-10, 13, 21).

Peter's boldness and courage were not produced in the energy of the flesh. The pre-Pentecostal, impetuous Peter would only have provoked the anger of the Council. It was the special, sudden filling with the Holy Spirit that produced the good result. The enemies of Christ were powerless in their opposition to one Spirit-filled man of God. The fullness of the Spirit for Peter on that occasion was not for the preaching of a great sermon. Two sermons had previously resulted in 8000 converts (Acts 2:41; 4:4). The filling in this instance enabled Peter to present with tact, boldness, and power a strong defense of his ministry.

When Peter and John were released, they immediately joined the other disciples and reported on their experience with the chief priest and elders. After listening to their testimony, the entire group joined in a service of praise and prayer, asking God for special boldness to speak His Word (Acts 4:23-30). "And when they had prayed, the place was shaken where they were assembled together; and they were all *filled with the Holy Ghost,* and they spake the word of God with boldness" (Acts 4:31). The stand the disciples took was not an exhibition of pride; it was not an ugly defiance of the enemies of Christ. They were men under the full control of the Holy Spirit. The wholesome results of the fullness of the Spirit could not be denied. They witnessed with boldness, souls were continually being saved, and the opposition was subdued.

Even the ordinary service by ordinary Christians demanded that those who performed the service be filled with the Spirit. When, in the early church, there was need of men to handle those mundane matters — such as managing finances and looking after the needy — only Spirit-filled men were chosen for the work. "Wherefore, brethren, look ye out among you seven men of honest report, *full of the Holy Ghost* and wisdom, whom we may appoint over this business" (Acts 6:3).

Deacons, elders, musicians, singers, youth and educational directors, and Sunday school teachers should be filled with the Spirit before attempting any service for the Lord. More than fifty years ago the late C. I. Scofield said, "No Christian should perform the slightest act in the service of Christ until he is definitely filled with the Holy Ghost." The way the early church solved its problems presents valuable lessons for the church of today. Let all preachers and Christian workers learn the lesson well — "Be filled with the Spirit."

Fifth, the Spirit's fullness equips the child of God for any and every emergency including persecution, suffering, and sacrifice. Those who neglect the study of all the Scriptures which deal with the Spirit's fullness associate the experience with speaking in tongues, emotional demonstrations, and large numbers of people in charismatic gatherings. All such persons should read and examine carefully Acts 7.

Stephen was the first recorded martyr in the Christian church. He was not delivered from the hands of the enemy, as were Peter and John, but died a cruel death. He was first recognized as a man full of the Holy Spirit at the time the Twelve were seeking men to assist them (Acts 6:3-5). For a brief time Stephen did perform great miracles among the people (Acts 6:8). But like Peter and John, Stephen was brought to trial before the rulers. This afforded him the opportunity to deliver that magnificent message recorded in Acts 7:1-53. But this time the reaction of the civil leaders was not the same as in the case of Peter and John. In hot anger they stoned him to death. Then Stephen, "being *full of the Holy*

85

Ghost, . . . kneeled down, and cried with a loud voice, Lord, lay not this sin to their charge" (Acts 7:55, 60). The Spirit's fullness fitted Stephen to die triumphantly. Victorious dying is a consequence of being filled with the Spirit. There is an ultimate relation between sufferings and being Spirit-filled.

Sixth, the Spirit's fullness enables the child of God to withstand satanic opposition. It was a crisis hour for the infant church when Paul and Silas went forth on their first missionary journey. When they arrived at Paphos, they encountered a sorcerer named Elymas. God knew that in order for His servants to combat that child of Satan, they would need a special filling of the Holy Spirit.

Luke records the events. "Then Saul, (who also is called Paul,) *filled with the Holy Ghost,* set his eyes on him, And said, O full of all subtilty and all mischief, thou child of the devil, thou enemy of all righteousness, wilt thou not cease to pervert the right ways of the Lord? And now, behold, the hand of the Lord is upon thee, and thou shalt be blind, not seeing the sun for a season. And immediately there fell on him a mist and a darkness; and he went about seeking some to lead him by the hand. Then the deputy, when he saw what was done, believed, being astonished at the doctrine of the Lord" (Acts 13:9-12). Paul's words were uncompromising, and his pronouncement of judgment might seem harsh to us. Nevertheless we well remember that Paul spoke and acted under the control of the Holy Spirit. He was dealing with a demon-possessed man, and therefore a special filling with the Holy Spirit was needed.

If the very apostles of our Lord — men whom He chose and trained — needed the mighty filling with the Holy Spirit, how much greater is that need in us! The Spirit's fullness is the indispensable experience in every Christian's life. In these days of stepped-up demonic activity, we need to be under the control of the Holy Spirit.

Seventh and last, the most wholesome result of the fullness of the Spirit is Christlikeness. The ministry of the Spirit is for the purpose of glorifying Christ, not Himself, and certainly none of us. Jesus said, "Howbeit when he, the Spirit of truth is come, . . . He shall glorify me: for he shall receive of mine, and shall shew it unto you" (John 16:13, 14). "He shall testify of me" (John 15:26).

It is common to hear people talking about the Holy Spirit and their own experiences, almost to the exclusion of Jesus Christ. The Holy Spirit imparts Christ's life to us and glorifies Christ in us. It was the mission of the Son to glorify the Father, and it is the mission of the Spirit to glorify the Son. Not that the Holy Spirit can add anything to the divine and personal glories which are Christ's; but the Holy Spirit glorifies the Lord Jesus in our hearts and in our daily living in order that people on earth might see His glory.

The test of any religious movement or personal experience is the place it gives to the person of Jesus Christ. The Holy Spirit does not promote Himself; He gives preeminence to the Lord Jesus. His ministry is Christocentric. And if we are Spirit-controlled, there will be practical manifestations of the lordship of Christ in our lives. The Holy Spirit is not content with anything less.

Study Questions

1. Contrast *carnality* and *spirituality*.
2. What does it mean to be "filled" with the Spirit?
3. Distinguish between the "filling" and the "baptism" with the Spirit.
4. What are the conditions for being filled with the Spirit?
5. What fallacies must be avoided in order to be filled with the Spirit?
6. What seven consequences result from being filled with the Holy Spirit?

Chapter 7

The Faction Between the Holy Spirit and the Flesh

> For the flesh lusteth against the Spirit, and the Spirit against the flesh: and these are contrary the one to the other: so that ye cannot do the things that ye would (Gal. 5:17).

This text is written against the background of a struggle within the believer. That struggle is a conflict between the Holy Spirit and that which the apostle calls "the flesh." Paul knew from his personal experience the torments of this conflict. We will examine his testimony later when we look at Romans 7.

The focus of this present chapter is *holiness*, that quality of life to which the Scriptures call all God's children. Frankly, I am at a loss to describe or define adequately exactly what holiness is. But I am convinced that the biblical idea of holiness contains both an ethical and a moral contest. It is associated with character and behavior.

We must refer to the Old Testament for the first gleam of God's view of holiness. God had said to His people, "Ye shall be holy; for I am holy" (Lev. 11:44). And again, "Ye shall be holy: for I the LORD your God am holy" (Lev. 19:2). He reiterated this command to His children in Leviticus 20:7, 26.

In the New Testament we discover the same truth. The apostle Peter wrote, "But as he which hath called you is holy, so be ye holy in all manner of conversation; Because it is written, Be ye holy; for I am holy" (1 Peter 1:15, 16). If I am correct in my assumption that holiness relates to character and behavior, morally and ethically, then God is saying to us who are His children, "Your character and behavior shall correspond to my character and behavior." Christian holiness is Godlikeness.

Someone may ask, "If the holiness God requires of us is Godlikeness, then we should rise in this life to the point of sinless perfection." My only answer for the present is that nowhere does the New Testament promise complete sinlessness in this life, yet it does teach true holiness. I shall not presume beyond what the Bible teaches, or more accurately, what I understand the teaching of Scripture to be. I believe holiness implies separation to God and the resultant conduct befitting those who are separated. For the want of a clearer term, I shall call Christian holiness *moral likeness to God*.

Man, as God created him, was essentially like God in his moral nature. God had said, "Let us make man in our image, after our likeness. . . . So God created man in his own image, in the image of God created he him" (Gen. 1:26, 27). We know that man did not retain his moral likeness to God. When he chose to sin, the divine image was marred. And so the first man, Adam, passed on to his posterity a nature devoid of the holiness of God. "Wherefore, as by one man sin entered into the world, and death by sin; and so death passed upon all men, for that all have sinned" (Rom. 5:12). Like begets like. All life reproduces after its kind; so "if we say that we have no sin, we deceive ourselves, and the truth is not in us" (1 John 1:8).

Included in the divinely planned redemptive process is the restoration of the divine image in man. We should not fail to see the central fact that, in this matter of holiness, God is at work. I am not suggesting that there is no human responsibility on the Christian's part. Indeed there is! Yet, as another has said, "Let this be axiomatic to all our thinking about holiness, that *whatever* spiritual change is wrought within us is the work of the Holy Spirit. . . . With that in mind, we may find it helpful at this point to draw certain definite lines of differentiation between the work of Christ and the work of the Holy Spirit in relation to Christian believers. In order to become eternally saved, we sinful human beings needed certain big things done *for* us, and certain vital changes wrought *in* us. By way of general differentiation we may say: it is God the Son who has effected all that needed doing *for* us; it is God the Holy Spirit who effects all that needs doing *in* us! Our Lord's work *for* us covers all the *judicial* aspects of our salvation. The Holy Spirit's work *in* us covers all the *experiential* aspects of it." More of this will follow when we consider precisely what the Holy Spirit does.

Look once more at the text of this chapter:

> For the flesh lusteth against the Spirit, and the Spirit against the flesh: and these are contrary the one to the other: so that ye cannot do the things that ye would (Gal. 5:17).

THE FOE OF HOLINESS

The enemy opposing holiness is called here "the flesh." The term *flesh* appears frequently in the writings of Paul, not less than 90 times. The Greek word is *sarx,* and it has a wide range of meaning in the New Testament. The adjectives *carnal* (Gr. *sarkikos)* and *fleshly* (Gr. *sarkinos)* appear also in the New Testament, though much less frequently than the noun *flesh.*

What is meant by this New Testament term "in the flesh"? More than 30 times it is used of the physical body, that is, the substance of the body, whether of beasts or the human body of men. This is the usage in the following passage: "All flesh is not the same flesh: but there is one kind of flesh of men, another flesh of beasts, another of fishes, and another of birds" (1 Cor. 15:39). I draw attention to this verse merely to point out the varied use of the word *flesh.* It is not used in this sense in Galatians 5:17.

When the word *flesh* is used in a theological or ethical sense, it refers to the seat of sin in man, that element in human nature which is evil in God's sight. Our Lord described it as being "weak" (Matt. 26:41). Paul was given to see it as having an "infirmity" (Rom. 6:19). "So then they that are in the flesh cannot please God" (Rom. 8:8). All natural efforts and attainments on the part of man, independent of the Holy Spirit, cannot please God and are therefore not acceptable to Him.

Paul raised the question, "What shall we say then that Abraham our father, as pertaining to the flesh, hath found?" (Rom. 4:1). In substance he was asking, "What did Abraham get in his own strength and by his own efforts, independent of God?" The answer is, Nothing! He was not justified by the flesh apart from God. Paul asked a similar question of the Galatians: "Are ye so foolish? having begun in the Spirit, are ye now made perfect by the flesh?" (Gal. 3:3). The idea is the same as in the preceding question. That is, "Having been born again by the power of the Holy Spirit, are you so foolish as to think that you can continue as a Christian by your own natural efforts, independent of the power of the Holy Spirit?" They needed to know that the flesh is weak and helpless, the dwelling place of "no good thing" (Rom. 7:18).

The meaning behind the expression *the flesh* in Galatians 5:17 is that selfish, self-centered propensity of our fallen human nature, the inclination to perversity. Someone has suggested the following: Drop the last letter, *h,* and then spell the remaining four letters backward. The result is *self.* The "flesh" is the total *self,* the whole man in his fallen, sinful, selfish state.

Adam as God created him was not self-centered. It was not until the Fall that he became so. Paul describes the human race in these terms: "Among whom also we all had our conversation [behavior] in times past in the lusts of our flesh, fulfilling the desires of the flesh and of the mind; and were by nature [our fallen, natural constitution] the children of wrath, even as others" (Eph. 2:3). The "flesh" here is that weak, sinful element in man's nature by reason of his descent from Adam. The flesh is the foe of holiness. "This I say then, Walk in the Spirit, and ye shall not fulfill the lust [the evil

desires] of the flesh [the self-centered propensity to evil]''
(Gal. 5:16).

It goes without my saying it that every believer experiences this inner conflict, the fighting between the flesh and the Spirit. Some of God's dear children know it to a lesser degree than do others. The Corinthian Christians, for example, were known for their carnality, not for spirituality. They were self-centered and self-controlled, not Spirit-controlled. Paul wrote to them and said, ''And I, brethren, could not speak unto you as unto spiritual, but as unto carnal, even as unto babes in Christ'' (1 Cor. 3:1). Those believers were fleshly, controlled by their selfish human nature. They were losers in the conflict, the flesh having them under control.

The adjective *spiritual* is a post-Pentecost word. It occurs neither in the Septuagint nor in the Gospels. When it is combined with the word *things,* as 1 Corinthians 2:13, 14, it refers to those things that have their origin with God, in harmony with God's nature and character. A carnal [or fleshly] person will say and do things that originate within themselves, that is, with their selfish, self-centered Adam nature. The carnal Christian is not under the control of the Holy Spirit. The spiritual Christian thinks, speaks, and acts under the control of the Holy Spirit, thus he is said to be spiritual.

But why are we not spiritual at all times and under all circumstances? The answer is clear to me. The flesh (that inherent evil in human nature) remains in us. It has not been eradicated, nor will it be in this present life. That inborn selfish urge, which is a part of our total humanity, continues to manifest itself. It has never been totally put to death experientially, certainly not in my own life. I believe that I have made some progress, but there is yet much work to be done. The warfare between the flesh and the Spirit continues, and I can find nothing in Scripture that assures me of its cessation.

When we Christians were born into the family of God, we became ''partakers of the divine nature'' (2 Peter 1:4), a fact confirmed by several New Testament passages. Paul says that the man in Christ is "a new creature [creation]" (2 Cor. 5:17). The divine nature is imparted to the believer in the person of the Holy Spirit, for all believers are indwelt by the Holy Spirit (see Rom. 5:5; 8:9; 1 Cor. 3:16; 6:19, 20). At the time of salvation we receive, through the Spirit's incoming, a new pull and new propensities toward holiness.

However, the Adamic nature is still with me. Shall I say that I now have two natures? There is a dear brother, whose personal friendship and gifted ministry I value highly; I hear him speak and read his books, always with pleasure and profit. He insists that the child of God does not have two natures, and yet he tells us that he is not an "eradicationist." Well, on that one matter we disagree. I know I became a partaker of the divine nature, and ever since my salvation experience there has been a growing desire and propensity toward holiness. But then (and it is now fifty years since I was born again), I know that the Adamic, fallen nature, with its inclinations to think, speak, and act in ways that are not holy, is still a part of me. Call these two diverse capacities what you will — two antagonists, two natures, two opposing forces; they are present in me and I am engaged in a day-by-day warfare. "The flesh lusteth against the Spirit, and the Spirit against the flesh." The foe of holiness is "the flesh."

THE FIGHT AGAINST HOLINESS

The fight against holiness is carried on by a threefold enemy: the *world,* the *flesh,* and the *devil.* If we are to be victorious in the combat, we must know the enemy and his strategy. We have examined in this chapter some Scriptures that describe the flesh and declare it to be an enemy of holiness. From this point on we examine what Paul calls "the works of the flesh."

What a person does bears testimony to what he is. This is true whether the "works" are good or evil. God is known by His works (John 10:37,38). Satan's character is manifested in his works (John 8:41). The character of Satan's ministers is revealed in their works (2 Cor. 11:15). The motives of the scribes and Pharisees were disclosed in their works (Matt.

23:1-3). The legalist is known by his works, called "the works of the law" (Gal. 3:2).

The Galatians had become victims of legalism. They were told by the legalizers that it was necessary to add "the works of the law" to faith in Christ, arguing that there could be no growth in the Christian life apart from obedience to the law of Moses. Paul challenges this false reasoning (Gal. 3:2, 3), and then he reminds them "that no man is justified by the law in the sight of God" (3:11). Since they became God's children by faith, and not by works, they dare not revert to the law as a means of practical, progressive sanctification. They could never bring themselves to spiritual maturity through self-effort. So he writes, "Stand fast therefore in the liberty wherewith Christ hath made us free, and be not entangled again with the yoke of bondage" (5:1).

This sound doctrinal teaching which Paul gave had in it a potential danger. It was always possible that some opponent of the pure doctrine of grace might deliberately read into Paul's argument something like this: "If the law no longer controls me, then all restraints are removed and I may live as I please. I may do whatever my desires and emotions tell me to do."

Paul will now answer this ridiculous reasoning. He will show that living selfishly will not save a man; it will destroy him. The man who lives to please himself fights against the Holy Spirit and therefore against holiness. Christian liberty does not mean that the Christian is free to indulge in the lusts of the flesh. The Christian who walks by means of the Spirit will not fulfill the lusts of the flesh (Gal. 5:16). The Christian is free, not to walk by means of the flesh, but in the power of the Holy Spirit. He who yields to the fallen Adamic nature fights against holiness.

The following is a list of evil things called "the works of the flesh" (Gal. 5:19). We have mentioned "the lust of the flesh." There is a difference between the *lust* of the flesh and the *works* of the flesh. The former term *(lust)* in verse 16 describes the inner propensities and desires of man in his fallen Adamic condition. The latter term *(works)* describes the surrender of the will to those desires. The works can be displayed in thought, in word, or in deed. Each word which forms a part of the works of the flesh must be examined separately.

Adultery may be defined as an act of illicit sex between married persons. God wrote clearly into His law, "Thou shalt not commit adultery" (Exod. 20:14). Here is an evil to which all normal persons are peculiarly susceptible. It was of special interest to me when I observed that this sin was placed at the head of the list of sensual sins. The Spirit-controlled Christian will not succumb to this evil. Adultery is a work of the flesh, a sin committed by carnally minded people. David was not walking by means of the Spirit when he engaged in adultery with Bathsheba. Adulterers and adulteresses are the enemies of God (James 4:4) and will therefore be judged by God (Heb. 13:4).

Fornication is the same sin as adultery when engaged in by unmarried persons. Chastity is one of the virtues which Christianity has magnified. The message of Christ's gospel has changed entire communities where, before the message was received, sexual immorality was condoned. Like adultery, fornication is a demoralizing practice. It is a work of the flesh.

Uncleanness has been defined as a general condition of impurity of mind. It is not uncommon to meet persons who appear to have a "dirty" mind; their words and actions betray them as being sensual and immorally suggestive. The Greek word the Holy Spirit uses is *akatharsia*. It has been used of the pus from an unclean sore or wound. The heart of the unclean person is soiled, thereby making him unfit to worship God. He needs a *katharos*, that cleansing which will make him fit to approach God. Filthiness of heart and mind defile a person marking him as one controlled by the flesh, not by the Holy Spirit. "Unto the pure all things are pure; but unto them that are defiled and unbelieving is nothing pure; but even their mind and conscience is defiled" (Titus 1:15).

Lasciviousness is lewdness. The Greek word Paul uses *(aselgeia)* is translated in the King James Version by the two words *lasciviousness* (Mark 7:22; 2 Cor. 12:21; Gal. 5:19; Eph. 4:19; 1 Peter 4:3; Jude 4) and *wantonness* (Rom. 13:13; 2 Peter 2:18). The lascivious person has an insolent disregard for decency, knows no restraint, is without shame, and is ready to engage in any practice the fallen nature might suggest. He is carried away by the lust of the flesh to the extent that he ceases to care what people think or say. These first four works of the flesh — *adultery, fornication, uncleanness, lasciviousness* — we may list as sensual sins.

Idolatry has had an incorrect connotation attached to it by modern-day Christians. It is usually looked upon merely as the worship of images, idols, medallions, and the like, things made by the hands of men. This meaning is not totally incorrect, but it is too limiting. Actually idolatry is the sin in which material things take the place of God. The Epistle to the Galatians was written to Christians; this tells us that a Christian can become involved in the sin of idolatry. Any Christian who is in bondage to material things in an idolater. When Paul wrote to the Christians, he said that "the covetous man . . . is an idolater" (Eph. 5:5) and that "covetousness . . . is idolatry" (Col. 3:5). The Christian idolater is in bondage to the depraved idea that things are more important than loving and serving Christ. Christian, beware! Idolatry is one of the "works of the flesh."

Witchcraft. The word Paul used is *pharmakia*, from which came our English word *pharmacy*. It has been used generally in connection with drugs, whether helpfully by medical science or harmfully by someone with evil intent. In Scripture it is used in a bad sense, of the enchantments or witchcraft of the Egyptians (Exod. 7:11, 22) and the sorceries of the Babylonians (Isa. 47:9, 12). Among ancient pagan peoples, drugs were used to accompany an appeal to occult forces; however, witchcraft and sorcery are sometimes practiced without the use of drugs. Whether accompanied by drugs or not, it is an evil practice forbidden by God (Deut. 18:9-22) and is definitely one of the "works of the flesh." It seems clear from Revelation 9:21 and 18:23 that this forbidden evil will flourish in the last days immediately preceding the coming again of Christ to the earth. These two "works of the flesh," *idolatry* and *witchcraft*, one might label *religious sins*.

Hatred is the Greek word *echthra*, a trait characteristic in the unregenerate man, making him hostile to his fellow men. It is the direct opposite of Christian love, showing itself in animosity and enmity. In the Greek text the word is plural. I am not certain why it appears in the plural number; however, it could indicate its association with the works of the flesh which follow: (1) *variance*, an expression of enmity showing itself in discord; (2) *emulations*, referring to jealousy; (3) *wrath*, that hostile feeling which shows itself in uncontrolled outbursts of anger — When one allows jealousy to smolder in the heart, it will break out in wrath; (4) *strife*, suggesting the idea of self-seeking, selfishness, factiousness; (5) *seditions*, or divisions — that work of the flesh which pulls apart and creates schism and cliques in the church; (6) *heresies*, which is the disastrous result of the preceding "works of the flesh." In its original use it did not have a bad connotation, but meant "to choose"; however, in the context in which it appears here, the choice to split the church grew out of a display of the flesh. Differing views were not settled agreeably, but resulted in men's choosing sides for or against, and this led to sectarianism; (7) *envyings* — to carry a grudge. I consider envy a serious spiritual sickness, because a proverb puts it, "Envy the rottenness of the bones" (Prov. 14:30). This is one of the nastier sins of the flesh.

These eight sins — hatred, variance, emulations, wrath, strife, seditions, heresies, envyings — contributed to the disgrace and downfall of the church at Corinth (1 Cor. 3:1-4). Not only is the believer to guard against committing them, but he is to avoid those persons who do (Rom. 16:17). These sins, like all the other "works of the flesh," fight against the Holy Spirit and holiness.

Three more sins are in the list in Galatians 5:19-21: *murder, drunkenness, revellings*. These three are closely related. Indulgence in strong drink can turn a man into a wild beast, a murderer. It will lead him into unrestrained and uncontrolled bad behavior. He will act like a fool.

Here, then, are eleven sins called "the works of the flesh." Is the fallen, Adamic nature capable of producing those horrible sins? Yes, it is. The flesh is the foe of holiness. It is not subject to the law of God (Rom. 8:7), nor can it ever please God (Rom. 8:8), because it is the dwelling place of no good thing (Rom. 7:18). As Christians we are under no obligation to the flesh, but to the Holy Spirit (Rom. 8:12-14). We must make no provision for it (Rom. 13:14), nor should we put confidence in it (Phil. 3:3). "This I say then, Walk in [by means of] the Spirit, and ye shall not fulfil the lust of the flesh" (Gal. 5:16).

Are you among those who have been fighting against the Holy Spirit? Are you guilty of any of the "works of the flesh"? If you are, then heed God's call to repent; confess and forsake your sin. The Holy Spirit will enable you to overcome the flesh.

Study Questions

1. What is Christian holiness, and why is it not the same as sinlessness?
2. Explain the ethical use of the term flesh in relation to holiness.
3. Why do Christians not behave spiritually at all times?
4. What is the threefold enemy of holiness?
5. Contrast the terms "lust of the flesh" and "works of the flesh."
6. Describe some of the eleven works of the flesh listed in Galatians 5:19-21.

Chapter 8

The Fruit of the Holy Spirit

"But the fruit of the Spirit is love, joy, peace, longsuffering, gentleness, goodness, faith, meekness, temperance: against such there is no law" (Gal. 5:22, 23).

An amazing fact concerning a genuine Christian experience is the clear teaching of the Bible that God Himself, in the person of the Holy Spirit, comes to dwell in the body of every saved person. That the God who created heaven and earth should condescend to take up His abode in me is indeed a wonder of astonishing proportions.

In my travels throughout America and abroad, I have seen elaborate and costly edifices erected to various gods for the purpose of worship. The remains of some of the ancient temples can be seen to this day. But every time I gaze upon one of them I am reminded of the words of the apostle Paul, who affirmed, "God that made the world and all things therein, seeing that he is Lord of heaven and earth, dwelleth not in temples made with hands" (Acts 17:24). God has deigned to dwell in the temple of the human heart. "And because ye are sons, God hath sent forth the Spirit of his Son into your hearts, crying, Abba, Father" (Gal. 4:6).

I remind you that in this tremendous spiritual truth there is a pregnant, expulsive power. Do not err by accepting this truth in a mere theological and theoretical sense. There are a number of practical reasons why the Father sent the Holy Spirit to dwell in our bodies. When Paul was led to write about one phase of the Holy Spirit's work in the Christian, he spoke of that work as "the fruit of the Spirit."

The Meaning of Fruit

Consider the word *fruit*. What does it suggest to you? Let me tell you what it does *not* suggest to me. It does not so much as hint at the idea of any work or effort on my part. There is an important and impressive contrast between *works* and *fruit*. When we think of works, our minds conceive of effort and toil on our part; when we think of fruit there comes to mind the product of a living organism, something produced by a power greater than ourselves.

In the spiritual realm, fruit can never be the results of human exertion and self-effort in order to obtain holiness. The fruit of the Spirit is the outward expression of God's power working in us. The lust of the flesh manifests itself in works. The Holy Spirit manifests His presence and power in His fruit. Any one of us may be theologically correct in the doctrine of the Holy Spirit, yet live a life that does not display the Spirit's fruit. The character of the fruit displays the character of the power that produced it.

The Scriptures speak of different kinds of fruit:

There is the *fruit of converts,* people who are won to Christ. This was the motivation behind Paul's desire to go to Rome (Rom. 1:13): he wanted to see fruit among them. (See also Phil. 1:22.)

There is the *fruit of conduct*. "But now being made free from sin, and become servants to God, ye have your fruit unto holiness, and the end everlasting life" (Rom. 6:22).

There is the *fruit of contribution*. These are our gifts given in the name of the Lord for the blessing and benefit of other of God's children. This is the fruit of which Paul wrote in Romans 15:26-28.

There is the *fruit of caring* for God's servants who labor in the gospel. The Philippian Christians had sent support for Paul. Acknowledging that support, he wrote, "Not because I desire a gift: but I desire fruit that may abound to your account" (Phil. 4:17).

There is the *fruit of confession.* "By him therefore let us offer the sacrifice of praise to God continually, that is, the fruit of our lips giving thanks to his name" (Heb. 13:15). The marginal reading renders this "confessing to his name."

The negative word *unfruitful* is used frequently in the New Testament to sound a warning to Christians. When we fail to obey God's Word, that word becomes unfruitful (unproductive) in our lives (Matt. 13:22). Then in turn, *we* become unfruitful (unproductive) (2 Peter 1:8). We are warned against having "fellowship with the unfruitful works of darkness" (Eph. 5:11).

But in Galatians 5:22, 23 the "fruit of the Spirit" has to do with *character.* The *fruit* must not be confused with the *gift* of the Spirit, which is salvation, nor with the *gifts* of the Spirit, which are for service. The fruit of the Spirit constitutes the graces of the Spirit. Today much stress is put upon the *gifts* of the Spirit to the neglect of the *graces* of the Spirit. The church at Corinth, which was the charismatic church, could demonstrate the gifts (1 Cor. 1:7), but did not display the graces. There was much function but "not fruit," when there should have been "fruit . . . more fruit . . . much fruit" (John 15:2, 5).

As we approach the text which sets forth the fruit of the Spirit (Gal. 5:22, 23), we must not overlook the fact that the word *fruit* is in the singular form. Several writers have penned their views as to why the singular form is used. If I am correct in my assumption that to be Spirit-filled is to be Christlike, then I prefer the following paragraph, taken from the Commentary on Galatians by Hogg and Vine, giving their explanation for the use of the singular form: "The singular form, 'fruit,' is used here perhaps to suggest the unity and harmony of the character of the Lord Jesus which is to be reproduced in the believer by the power of the Holy

103

Spirit, in contrast with the discordant and often mutually antagonistic 'works of the flesh.' In Christ actually, and in the Christian potentially, the fruit of the Spirit is harmonious, the various elements being mutually consistent, and each encouraging and enhancing the rest in happy co-ordination and co-operation in that 'new man, which after God hath been created in righteousness and holiness of truth' (Eph. 4:24)."

The nine elements, or graces, constitute a unit, providing for a complete and full Christian life. Let us examine them.

THE MANIFESTATION OF THE FRUIT

Love. In Greek there are a number of different words for love: (1) *Eros* means the love that is expressed in sex relations. It can be the love of a man for a woman and vice versa; this is physical and involves sexual love. When used by homosexuals, God calls it "vile affections" (Rom. 1:26). *Eros* is never used in the New Testament; (2) *Phileo* is the love that we show toward our fellow men; a philanthropist is a person who loves and helps mankind; (3) *Storge* is that wholesome affection that parents have for their children; it is the word for family love; (4) *Agape* is the particular word for love which Paul used in Galatians 5:22; it means divine love, the very nature of God. "God is love" (1 John 4:8, 16). It is that seed of divine love which is sown in the heart of the believer the moment he becomes God's child. "The love of God is shed abroad in our hearts by the Holy Ghost which is given unto us" (Rom. 5:5). *Agape* is a word peculiar to Christianity.

This first-mentioned fruit of the Spirit is an all-embracing love. In this it differs radically from ordinary human love: we humans do not love people we don't like. But God loves every human (John 3:16) simply because He is "the God of love" (2 Cor. 13:11). He proved His love completely and fully, for it was while we were still sinners that Christ died for us (Rom. 5:8). The whole process of salvation originated in the unmerited love of God. This love is so strong that nothing in time or in eternity can separate a child of God from it

104

(Rom. 8:35-39). Paul referred to it as "His [God's] great love" (Eph. 2:4), "which passeth knowledge" (Eph. 3:19), meaning that it is something which cannot be fully explained, only experienced and expressed.

I am not surprised that this cluster of fruit begins with love.

Love is The Christian *characteristic* (1 Cor. 13:13).
Love is The Christian *commandment* (John 15:12).
Love is The Christian's *constraint* (2 Cor. 5:14).
Love is The Christian's *controller* (1 Cor. 16:14; Gal. 5:13).
Love is The Christian's *clothing* (Col. 3:14).
Love is The Christian's *covering* (1 Peter 4:8).

The love Paul speaks of, this fruit of the Spirit, will always seek the highest good of others. It is unselfish, never self-seeking. Humanly speaking it is impossible; it is not a human achievement. It springs to life in us only as we are controlled by the Holy Spirit. And when He is in control of our lives, we will "increase and abound in love one toward another, and toward all men" (1 Thess. 3:12), and "love one another with a pure heart fervently" (1 Peter 1:22).

Millions of people watched on television in July 1975 the match race between horses, Ruffian and Foolish Pleasure. They sat in stunned silence when the filly Ruffian came to an abrupt halt, having broken her leg. When it was known that the horse had to be destroyed, every major network presented the news of the death of the horse as a great tragedy. Millions of Americans mourned the death of an animal.

In the same newscast there was a mere mention of the fact that a thirteen-year-old girl was raped and murdered. This is a commentary on our times and brings home the tragic truth that we live in a loveless world. Life has become highly impersonal; most of us care about ourselves. May God help us Christians to walk by means of the Spirit and not fulfill the lust of the flesh.

Joy. Christian joy is a fruit of the Holy Spirit independent of circumstances. It is a distinguishing characteristic of the Christian life. Someone has said that the word *rejoice* is the standing-order of the Christian: whatever else the early Christians were told to do, the exhortation to rejoice headed the

105

list. "Finally, my brethren, rejoice in the Lord" (Phil. 3:1). "Rejoice in the Lord alway; and again I say, Rejoice" (4:4). "Rejoice evermore" (1 Thess. 5:16). A joyless life is not the true Christian life. Neither outward circumstances nor people can effect this fruit of the Spirit.

When I examine the many references to joy in the New Testament, I am deeply impressed with the various spheres of Christian experience with which joy is associated. The grounds of joy were many. Every event in the life of our Lord Jesus Christ was accompanied with joy. When the angel announced to Mary the news concerning the child she was to bear, he greeted her with a benediction of joy (Luke 1:28). At Christ's birth it was "good tidings of great joy" the angel brought to the shepherds (Luke 2:10). When the wise men saw the star which told them of the King's birth, "they rejoiced with exceeding great joy" (Matt. 2:10). When Christ healed the woman who had an infirmity for eighteen years, "all the people rejoiced for all the glorious things that were done by him" (Luke 13:17). As He looked forward to His own death, He did so with joy (Heb. 12:2). On the morning of our Lord's resurrection the women returned from the tomb with "great joy" (Matt. 28:8). The ascension of Christ gave to the disciples "great joy" (Luke 24:52). He had told them that if they loved Him they would rejoice when He returned to the Father (John 14:28).

Other references in the New Testament tell us that there is no circumstance and no occasion that is not made radiant with joy. A joyless life does not reflect a genuine Christian experience. The preaching of the gospel and the exposition of God's Word were an occasion for joy (Acts 8:8, 39; 13:48; Phil. 1:18; 1 Thess. 1:6). There is joy in heaven every time a sinner repents and is converted (Luke 15:3-10). When we Christians cannot rejoice at the sound of God's Word and the changes His Word produces in the lives of others, it is a sure indication that we are not filled with the Spirit. The further the gospel spreads and the more who hear and receive it, the greater should be our joy. Let us never forget that one of the objects of preaching and teaching the Christian message is to

106

bring joy (John 15:11; 17:13; 2 Cor. 1:24; Phil. 1:25).

I believe that one of the greatest of all joys will be the joy we shall experience in heaven when we meet those whom we have brought to Jesus Christ. Paul's converts, both in Philippi and Thessalonica, were his joy and crown (Phil. 4:1; 1 Thess. 2:19, 20). If we are faithful in our stewardship here, we will be able to give a good account with joy at that day (Heb. 13:17).

This fruit of the Spirit is a completely new experience for the Christian, expressing itself anew even in times of affliction and sorrow. What do we know about joy in the midst of tribulation? Most of us express joy when all is well and things are going as we planned. In times of persecution "the disciples were filled with joy, and with the Holy Ghost" (Acts 13:52). You see, the two experiences — being filled with the Holy Spirit and filled with joy — go hand in hand. Paul testified that he was "sorrowful, yet alway rejoicing" (2 Cor. 6:10). The Thessalonian Christian "received the word in much affliction, with joy of the Holy Ghost" (1 Thess. 1:6). The saints in the churches of Macedonia, while experiencing "a great trial of affliction" showed forth "the abundance of their joy" (2 Cor. 8:1, 2). To the unconverted it is a strange paradox, this matter of joy in tribulation; but to the Spirit-filled child of God it is a real and wonderful thing. It is the fruit of the Spirit.

Peace. There are few things for which men have longed for as much as peace. Peace is one of the truly great words in the Bible. The Greek word is *eirene,* and it conveys the idea of right relationships.

Peace describes the right relationship between God and man. However, peace always originates with God. The Bible calls it "the peace of God" (Phil. 4:7; Col. 3:15), because He is "the God of peace," a title mentioned no fewer than six times (Rom. 15:33; 16:20; 2 Cor. 13:11; Phil. 4:9; 1 Thess. 5:23; Heb. 13:20). It is not possible for us humans to achieve this peace; it is something we must accept. God makes it available to us through His Son. Though it is one of God's richest gifts offered freely to all, many do not possess it. This right relationship between God and man, Christ established through His death, "having made peace through the blood of his cross" (Col. 1:20).

I once heard an evangelist appeal to his audience with these words, "Make your peace with God." But no person can make his peace with God; this is humanly impossible. The estrangement between God and man is the result of man's sin, and not until the debt of sin was paid could the sinner have peace with God. "Therefore being justified by faith, we have peace with God through our Lord Jesus Christ" (Rom. 5:1).

Peace describes the right relationship between men. The Christian is not merely a peace-taker; he is a peacemaker. Jesus said, "Blessed are the peacemakers" (Matt. 5:9). It is enjoined upon every Christian to strive for peace with his fellow men. "If it be possible, as much as lieth in you, live peaceably with all men" (Rom. 12:18). "Follow peace with all men" (Heb. 12:14). The troublemaker within the body of Christ is doing the work of the devil, and God will not hold such Christians guiltless. The disturbers of peace in the church are people walking after the flesh. Strife is a work of the flesh; peace is a fruit of the Spirit. Only the Spirit-filled Christian can "keep the unity of the Spirit in the bond of peace" (Eph. 4:3). The apostle Paul wrote, "Let the peace of God rule in your hearts" (Col. 3:15). The word *rule* was used of an umpire in sporting events and games. Our decisions are not to be determined by personal ambition or selfish gratifications, but rather "the peace of God" is to be the umpire of all decisions. The fruit of the Spirit is peace.

Longsuffering. This is an interesting word, expressing the idea of patience, spiritual endurance. It is an ingredient missing from the daily experience of too many Christians. Because of the weakness of the flesh, we are short-tempered and too frequently driven to despair. We become irritated too easily. This weakness shows up in our attitude toward both people and events. Some of us can retaliate a wrong hastily and at times with bitterness. William Barclay said, "If God had been a man He would have taken His hand and wiped out this world long ago; but God has that patience which bears with all our sinning and which will not cast us off." This living, forbearing fruit can be produced in the lives of Christians.

Longsuffering describes the nature and character of God. Moses heard God's description of Himself in these words: "The LORD God, merciful and gracious, longsuffering . . ." (Exod. 34:6). Nehemiah described Him as "God ready to pardon, gracious and merciful, slow to anger . . ." (9:17). The Psalms echo this amazing characteristic of God: "But thou, O Lord, art a God full of compassion, and gracious, longsuffering, and plenteous in mercy and truth" (86:15). "The Lord is merciful and gracious, slow to anger, and plentious in mercy" (103:8). "The Lord is gracious, and full of compassion; slow to anger, and of great mercy" (145:8). This is a great truth about God that we need to learn.

We who are the children of God, having received God's nature, should be displaying this lovely grace. We should be conducting ourselves as Jesus did, "who, when he was reviled, reviled not again; when he suffered, he threatened not; but committed himself to him that judgeth righteously" (1 Peter 2:23). It was Christ's longsuffering which was the basis of His forgiveness when He prayed for His enemies, "Father, forgive them; for they know not what they do" (Luke 23:34). That kind of praying for one's persecutors could never come from a bitter and impatient heart. A proverb says, "The discretion of a man deferreth his anger . . ." (Prov. 19:11). And again, "A wrathful man stirreth up strife; but he that is slow to anger appeaseth strife" (Prov. 15:18). The person whose temper is under control protects unity and fellowship among believers and will not permit strife to occur.

This needed and lovely fruit of the Spirit waits patiently when the impatient and short-tempered person has long since acted in divisive and sometimes destructive anger. Longsuffering is high on the list of Christian virtues. None of us can be a success in the Christian life without longsuffering. It is the fruit of the Spirit.

Gentleness. This beautiful word suggests the ideas of kindness and sweetness, possibly with the stronger emphasis on kindness. In the psalmist's description of God he used this term frequently: "O give thanks unto the LORD: for he is good [literally *kind*]: for his mercy endureth for ever" (Pss. 106:1; 107:1; 136:1). The word *good* here does not mean moral goodness, but kindness. The sheer kindness of God has gripped the heart of the psalmist. The gentleness of God is not a moral attribute; it is His kindness, that kindness which bestows His gifts upon us and draws us to Him. God's kindness is seen in all His dealings with men, whether they be saints or sinners. The psalmist appeals to men to "taste and see that the LORD is good [meaning gentle, kind]" (Ps. 34:8). "He is kind unto the unthankful and to the evil" (Luke 6:35).

We may expect, therefore, that we Christians, being indwelt by the Holy Spirit, will be displaying the fruit of gentleness and kindness. We know the value of a coin by the imprint on it; and we know that a person is a Spirit-filled child of God when we see the stamp of gentleness. This fruit of the Spirit identifies a person as belonging to God and controlled by God. One of the tragedies of life is that too few of us display this gentleness in the daily routine. Yet it is one of the garments of the well-dressed Christian. "Put on therefore, as the elect of God, holy and beloved, bowels of mercies, kindness, humbleness of mind, meekness, longsuffering" (Col. 3:12). The word *kindness* is the Greek word *chrestotes*, translated *gentleness* in Galatians 5:22.

Beloved Christian, when we are filled with the Spirit, the fruit of gentleness cannot be hidden. This lovely fruit banishes all bitterness, roughness, and harshness. It is a kindly thing which treats others as God has treated us. "Be ye kind one to another, . . . even as God for Christ's sake hath forgiven you" (Eph. 4:32).

Goodness. The Greek word Paul used is *agathosune*, a term not easy to define. One of the difficulties is in the wide and varied use of the corresponding adjective *agathos*. It has been pointed out that in the New Testament, this word is used to describe a gift (Matt. 7:11); a tree (Matt. 7:17, 18); a man

110

(Matt. 12:35); a slave (Matt. 25:21); fertile ground (Luke 8:8); a man's conscience (Acts 23:1); the will of God (Rom. 12:2); the Christian's hope (2 Thess. 2:16); the Christian's works (Eph. 2:10). At once we can see that goodness can and does describe what is excellent in any sphere of life. It is a general term.

The goodness which is the fruit of the Spirit we do not come by naturally. It is not consistent with our fallen, sinful nature. Paul confessed, "For I know that in me (that is, in my flesh), dwelleth no good thing . . ." (Rom. 7:18). "There is none that doeth good, no, not one" (Rom. 3:12). We must remember this when thinking about ourselves. It becomes an easy matter for us to pride ourselves in our own goodness, when in reality this fruit of the Spirit is the ingredient missing from our lives.

The wrong use of the term *goodness* has created serious problems. In recent years we have been confronted with the old relativism under the new title of "situational ethics." This is the old idea that all things are relative. We are told we should not lay down a set of rules, but rather we must wait for the situation to present itself and then decide whether a thing is good or bad. My answer to that theory is that man is not capable in himself to make such a decision, because "the heart is deceitful above all things, and desperately wicked . . ." (Jer. 17:9). The danger in situational ethics is that each man becomes a law unto himself. The children of Israel adopted that satanic system during the times of the Judges, when "every man did that which was right in his own eyes" (Judg. 17:6; 21:25). However, those days were some of the darkest in Israel's history, for "the children of Israel did evil in the sight of the LORD" (Judg. 2:11; 3:7, 12; 4:1; 6:1; 8:33; 10:6; 13:1). What seemed good in their eyes was bad in the sight of God. We must never forget, "There is a way which seemeth right unto a man, but the end thereof are the ways of death" (Prov. 14:12).

The Christian needs to be controlled by a power stronger than himself. That power is the power of almighty God made available to each believer as he yields to the control of the

111

Holy Spirit, "for the fruit of the Spirit is in all goodness . . ." (Eph. 5:9). Paul's prayer for the believers in Thessalonica was that God would bring to pass in them "every good word and work" (2 Thess. 2:17). Apparently the saints at Rome were manifesting the fruit of *goodness*. Paul wrote to them, "And I myself also am persuaded of you, my brethren, that ye also are full of goodness . . ." (Rom. 15:14). There must have been a number of Spirit-filled believers in that assembly. We could use.more of them today. "Be filled with the Spirit. . . . The fruit of the Spirit is goodness."

Faith. The seventh of the graces in the fruit of the Spirit is misleading in the King James Version. Careful consideration of the original text shows that a better translation would be *faithfulness*. It is the quality of reliability, dependability, trustworthiness, fidelity. A person on whom we can utterly rely and whose word we can utterly trust we call faithful. Faithfulness defines more clearly what Paul wrote when he said, "The fruit of the Spirit is faith."

Faithfulness is one of the essential attributes of God. Again and again we find this word in Scripture used to describe God. He is said to be faithful to His covenants (Deut. 7:9); He is faithful to His calling (1 Cor. 1:9; 1 Thess. 5:24); faithful in caring for His children when they are tried (1 Cor. 10:13); faithful to His creation (1 Peter 4:19); faithful in cleansing us when we confess our sins to Him (1 John 1:9). God's faithfulness remains constant despite the fickleness and faithlessness of men. *Faithful* is the adjective which characteristically describes God (Heb. 10:23; 11:11). Through many books of the Bible one finds the ever-recurring assuring word, "You can always count on God."

It is a word used to describe our Lord Jesus Christ. Jesus is the faithful witness (Rev. 1:5; 19:11): I will stake my life on the truth of everything He said. He is the faithful High Priest (Heb. 2:17): I can count on His keeping the way open to the Father and on His personal prayers in my behalf (Heb. 7:25). Dear reader, you can always depend on Jesus.

We are not to be surprised therefore to learn that this same virtue is expected in each Christian. God requires loyalty,

112

reliability from His children. "Moreover it is required in stewards, that a man be found faithful" (1 Cor. 4:2). This word is God's word of commendation to the faithful servants in the parable of the talents (Matt. 25:14-30). It was the lesson on loyalty and trustworthiness that Christ taught in the parable of the unjust steward (Luke 16:1-12). Repeatedly this word is used in the Epistles to describe those who are worthy of serving Christ (1 Cor. 4:17; Eph. 6:21; Col. 1:7; 4:9; 1 Peter 5:12; 3 John 5).

You can always depend on God. Can He count on you? The fruit of the Spirit is faithfulness.

Meekness. This is a much misunderstood word. Today the very sound of this word *meekness* suggests anemic spinelessness, a kind of weakness. With most people it is not a quality to be admired. Our Lord said of Himself, "I am meek and lowly in heart" (Matt. 11:29), yet He was not weak. When He overthrew the tables of the moneychangers and chased them from the temple, He displayed His power and authority, but it was power and authority under control. All Christ's words and actions were under divine control at all times. There never was a display of hot-headed temper.

Meekness is an extraordinarily beautiful and powerful Christian grace. It is like a soothing ointment that calms wherever it is applied. The meek Christian is a person who has learned to accept discipline and is therefore under the control of the Holy Spirit. He is trained in the fine art of obeying the commands of God's Word. He is strong, but his strength is combined to gentleness.

The meek person enjoys special blessings from God. There is the blessing of God's guidance and instruction: "The meek will he guide in judgment: and the meek will he teach his way" (Ps. 25:9). There is the blessing of a special inheritance: "The meek shall inherit the earth" (Ps. 37:11; Matt. 5:5). "For the LORD taketh pleasure in his people: he will beautify the meek with salvation" (Ps. 149:4).

Lowliness and meekness are characteristic of the Christian calling (Eph. 4:2). Meekness is a lovely piece of apparel that the well-dressed Christian will wear at all times (Col. 3:12).

113

Paul directed Titus that he should instruct the Christians to be "gentle, shewing all meekness unto all men" (Titus 3:2). If the Word of God is to be effective in our lives, it must be received by us with meekness (James 1:21). Even in our witness for Christ the grace of gentleness must be shown. A genuine Christian witness has always that sweet gentleness about it which is far more receptible than the rude type of witness which forces its views upon others. The apostle Peter wrote, "But sanctify the Lord God in your hearts: and be ready always to give an answer to every man that asketh you a reason of the hope that is in you with meekness and fear" (1 Peter 3:15).

Women are exhorted to adorn themselves with that "ornament of a meek and quiet spirit, which is in the sight of God of great price" (1 Peter 3:4). Meekness commends itself to God and to man. But we cannot produce it in our own strength; it is a part of the fruit of the Spirit. We all can do with a little more of it.

Temperance. This ninth and last-mentioned grace in the fruit of the Spirit can be translated *self-control.* It means to take hold of, to grip, to have under control, suggesting self-restraint, self-denial, self-discipline. In the moral and ethical sphere it describes the person who takes hold on himself, who has a grip on himself, is in full control of himself, so that he can restrain himself in all areas of life.

Peter exhorted his readers to add temperance to knowledge (2 Peter 1:6). Most of us know what we ought to do in matters pertaining to bodily pleasures, desires, and appetites, but too frequently we don't add self-control to that knowledge. Flagrant lack of self-control indicates carnality.

An athlete who seeks to win the contest will get himself in physical shape by being temperate in eating, sleeping, and exercising. Paul likened the Christian life to an athletic event, laying down the principle that every Christian who hopes to receive a reward will be "temperate in all things" (1 Cor. 9:25). Of course, he had in mind the care of the body. In the same epistle, when discussing celibacy and marriage, Paul speaks freely about the relationship between the sexes. He

114

seems to favor remaining unmarried, but then he adds, "If they cannot contain [that is, if self-control proves impossible], let them marry: for it is better to marry than to burn" (7:9). He makes it plain that a bishop must be a man of self-control (Titus 1:8). Intemperance is a work of the flesh and the enemy of the Holy Spirit. Temperance, or self-control, is a fruit of the Spirit.

I must warn you to beware of counterfeiting the fruit of the Spirit, putting on an outward show of spurious fruit. You have probably seen displays of artificial fruit. My wife and I were entertained for dinner in a home where the hostess had a dish of artificial fruit for the centerpiece; it looked so real one was tempted to pluck a grape from the bunch. But it was not to be eaten, only put on display to be admired. It was counterfeit. Such artificial fruit could never satisfy the hunger of a starving person.

Temperance is a virtue of the Spirit-filled Christian that makes him fit to serve God and bring blessing to his fellow men. Many are starving for want of love, joy, and peace. We are to be fruit-bearing Christians, not for our own good, but for the blessing and benefit of others. The Lord Jesus said, "Herein is my Father glorified, that ye bear much fruit; so shall ye be my disciples" (John 15:8). And remember that the nine graces are inseparable. To possess one is to have all. No one grace can of itself manifest the Holy Spirit if it is dissociated from the other graces in the list.

Study Questions

1. Why does the Scripture use the term "fruit" of the Spirit rather than "fruits"?
2. Distinguish between the four different Greek words for *love*.
3. Explain Christian joy.
4. How does *peace* explain our relationship with God and with other persons?
5. Choose three of the following fruit of the Spirit and explain them: longsuffering, gentleness, goodness, faithfulness, meekness, temperance.

115

Chapter 9

The Future Ministry of the Holy Spirit

The future ministry of the Holy Spirit is a phase of His activity that has failed to attract the attention of some theologians and Bible teachers. Even in some standard works on eschatology, the doctrine of the Holy Spirit is conspicuous by its absence. I have searched through a number of volumes and have found little consideration given to this aspect of the Spirit's activity.

One reason for this omission is the fact that neither the postmillennialist nor the amillennialist has a reason to consider any future ministry of the Holy Spirit on the earth. Even some premillennialists have done precious little with this subject. Being a premillennialist, I consider the subject an essential part of the doctrine of the Holy Spirit.

To develop our theme in an orderly and chronological sequence, it is helpful to consider the order of future events according to the prophetic Scriptures. The Bible predicts that the next event in God's prophetic program is the imminent return of Jesus Christ to gather His church to Himself. This event we call the Rapture (John 14:3; 1 Cor. 15:51, 52; 1 Thess. 4:16, 17). This appearance of Christ could occur at any time. I know of no prophecy that must be fulfilled prior to the Rapture.

After the church has been caught up to heaven, there follows a period of unprecedented trouble on the earth that will continue for approximately seven years. This is the Seventieth Week of Daniel's prophecy (Dan. 9:24-27). These seven years will be divided into two parts of three and one-half years each, the latter half called by the Lord, "great tribulation" (Matt. 24:21).

The purpose of the Tribulation is at least twofold. First, God will use it to prepare the nation Israel for the second advent of the Messiah to the earth. It is primarily Jewish (Deut. 4:30; Jer. 30:7; Dan. 12:1; Zech. 13:8, 9; Matt. 24:9-20). Second, during the Tribulation God will judge the unbelieving Gentiles (Isa. 26:21; Jer. 25:32, 33). This period closes abruptly with the return of Christ to the earth to set up His kingdom of earthwide peace and righteousness. This, in turn, is followed by the new heavens, the new earth, and the eternal state.

We are now faced with the question, What will be the Holy Spirit's function in those future dispensations? This question relates closely to another, namely, Will the Holy Spirit remain on the earth after the removal of the church?

Note 2 Thessalonians 2:7, 8: "For the mystery of iniquity doth already work: only he who now letteth will let, until he be taken out of the way. And then shall that Wicked [one] be revealed. . . ."

It had been circulated erroneously among the Christians in Thessalonica that they were already in the Tribulation, the day of the Lord. In order to correct this false idea Paul, inspired by the Holy Spirit, told them that they could not be in the day of the Lord because that day would not come until the Man of Sin had been revealed. Moreover, the appearance of Satan's Man on the earth was being prevented by a restraining power. Not until the restrainer was removed could the Man of Sin be presented.

It is true that the spirit of the Man of Sin — which is in reality the spirit which rejects the Lord Jesus Christ — was then "already in the world" (1 John 4:3). In the days of Christ's apostles there were actually false apostles and false prophets who, while presenting themselves as the apostles of Jesus Christ, were His declared enemies (2 Cor. 11:13-15; 1 John 2:18, 19, 22; 2 John 7). History will prove that every generation throughout the present dispensation of the church has had its precursors of Satan's Man of Sin. But that Man of Sin, the devil's instrument, will not appear to wage his final and formidable offensive as long as the restrainer remains on earth to prevent him.

Who is the restrainer? Not less than five answers have been offered to this question: (1) The Roman Empire with its unusual system of law and justice is the restrainer. Alexander Reese promoted this view in his book, *The Approaching Advent of Christ* (p. 246).

(2) Closely associated with Reese's view is that of Hogg and Vine, namely, the existing authorities of human government and law, being ordained of God, constitute the restrainer. Their thoughts are presented in the book they co-authored, *The Epistles of Paul the Apostle to the Thessalonians* (pp. 259-60).

(3) Satan is the restrainer. This view is (to me at least) furthest from the correct answer to our question. Why should Satan restrain his own Man of Sin? "If a house be divided against itself, that house cannot stand" (Mark 3:25). In the period following the church's removal, Satan's fury is unleashed on the earth; the removal of the restrainer does not free the earth from Satan's power, which would be the case if Satan were the restrainer.

(4) The church is the restrainer. Jesus did say to His disciples, "Ye are the salt of the earth" (Matt. 5:13), and since salt is both a purifier and a preservative, some writers believe that the church is the restraining influence to hold back the appearance of the Man of Sin. This seems unlikely, because the church is people, and we Christians who constitute the members of the church are imperfect as long as we are on the earth in these mortal bodies.

(5) The Holy Spirit is the restrainer. I share this view because I am convinced that the power which holds back the power of Satan must be greater than Satan's power; it must be

119

divine. We humans are no match for the one who possesses superhuman strength. Satan is a spirit-being who operates in the realm of the spirit-world; therefore the work of restraining evil must be confined to the Godhead.

Some commentators have difficulty with the idea that the Holy Spirit will function on the earth after the removal of the church. The Scripture says He will "be taken out of the way" (2 Thess. 2:7), meaning that He will be taken from the earth together with the church. This is clearly the case. The Spirit's departure from the earth at that time is supported by the fact that He resides in each Christian individually (Rom. 8:9; 1 Cor. 3:16; 6:19, 20) and in the church corporately (Eph. 2:21, 22). If He goes up to heaven together with the church, how then can He have a future ministry on the earth during the Tribulation?

It seems reasonable to assume that the Holy Spirit's influence will be greatly lessened on the earth following the Rapture. However, we must never forget that the Holy Spirit is omnipresent (Ps. 139:7); this means, of course, that He is present in all places. His operations on the earth after the church's departure should be much as they were in Old Testament times before His coming at Pentecost.

THE HOLY SPIRIT DURING THE TRIBULATION

There is a popular misconception in some religious circles, namely, that all persons who enter the Tribulation following the Rapture will be irrevocably lost. Those who hold to this view support it with the assertion that because the Holy Spirit has left the earth, it will be impossible for people to become saved. This idea is being preached by some as a leverage upon the unsaved. Now, it is true that there will be some persons alive on the earth at the time of the Rapture who will not be saved in the Tribulation. They are those who had heard the truth, but who willfully and knowingly rejected it (2 Thess. 2:10, 11). They had the truth but spurned it, therefore God will cause them to believe *the lie* because they preferred it. But there is nothing in the Thessalonian passage to indicate that no one will be saved.

On the other hand, great numbers will be saved during the Tribulation. The Holy Spirit's ministry does not cease at the Rapture. Early in the Tribulation period, God will seal 144,000 Jews; their sealing of necessity includes their salvation (Rev. 7:4-8). After the salvation of the 144,000 Jews, an innumerable multitude will turn to the Lord "of all nations, and kindreds, and people, and tongues" (Rev. 7:9). How do we know they are saved during the Tribulation? It is stated specifically that "These are they which came out of great tribulation, and have washed their robes, and made them white in the blood of the Lamb" (Rev. 7:14).

The passage in Revelation does not say what part the Holy Spirit will have in their conversion, though it would seem out of place to assume that He will have no part. Even before Pentecost Jesus said, "Except a man be born of . . . the Spirit, he cannot enter the kingdom of God" (John 3:5). There is no cessation of the Spirit's work in salvation during the Tribulation; Jews and Gentiles alike will be saved at that time.

The Old Testament prophets predicted a national salvation for Israel which would follow individual salvation. Speaking of the Tribulation, Jeremiah wrote, "Alas! for that day is great, so that none is like it: it is even the time of Jacob's trouble; but he shall be saved out of it" (30:7).

While Jeremiah does not mention any activity of the Holy Spirit in connection with Israel's salvation in the Tribulation, we do have a timely word from the prophet Joel. Note carefully this passage:

> And it shall come to pass afterward, that I will pour out my spirit upon all flesh; and your sons and your daughters shall prophesy, your old men shall dream dreams, your young men shall see visions: And also upon the servants and upon the handmaids in those days will I pour out my spirit. And I will shew wonders in the heavens and in the earth, blood, and fire, and pillars of smoke. The sun shall be turned into darkness, and the moon into blood, before the great and the terrible day of the LORD come. And it shall come to pass, that whosoever shall call on the name of the Lord shall be delivered: for in mount Zion and in Jerusalem shall be deliverance, as the

121

LORD hath said, and in the remnant whom the LORD shall call
(Joel 2:28-32).

In this passage the future salvation of Israel is related to the
ministry of the Holy Spirit. God said, "I will pour out my
spirit upon all flesh. . . ." On the day of Pentecost Peter
quoted the Joel passage. I do not know the total purpose for
this quotation in Acts 2:16-21, but I am certain that it did not
have a complete fulfillment at Pentecost. The passage in Acts
associates the pouring out of the Holy Spirit with that time
when "the sun shall be turned into darkness, and the moon
into blood" (Acts 2:20). Those activities in the heavens will
occur at the close of the Tribulation, even as our Lord stated
in Matthew 24:29, 30. These related Scriptures in Joel 2 and
Acts 2 indicate clearly a future ministry of the Holy Spirit in
Israel's behalf.

Ezekiel prophesied of that future work of the Holy Spirit in
behalf of Israel, a prediction that still awaits fulfillment after
the Rapture of the church. God showed Ezekiel a valley of
dry bones, and then said to him, "Son of man, these bones
are the whole house of Israel" (37:11). As Ezekiel stood
viewing the sight, God gave to him the great prophecy
concerning the regathering of the nation in her own land and
the spiritual rebirth of the people. "Thus saith the Lord GOD;
Behold, O my people, I will open your graves, and cause you
to come up out of your graves, and bring you into the land
of Israel. . . . And shall put my spirit in you, and ye shall
live . . ." (37:12, 14). These passages indicate clearly that
the restoration and regathering of the nation are in view, and
that the Holy Spirit is the agent accomplishing the work in the
hearts of the people. Those to whom the Holy Spirit comes
are the believing Jews who are saved during the Tribulation
and who survive to enter the kingdom at the second advent of
Christ.

Paul wrote of them, "And so all Israel shall be saved: as it
is written, There shall come out of Sion the Deliverer, and
shall turn away ungodliness from Jacob: For this is my
covenant unto them, when I shall take away their sins"

(Rom. 11:26, 27). Here the apostle speaks of Israel's national salvation spoken of by Ezekiel. She will be saved in the same manner as the apostle Paul was saved and as we Christians have been saved — by a revelation of the Lord Jesus Christ through the power of the Holy Spirit. Jesus said of the Holy Spirit, "He shall testify of me. . . . He shall glorify me" (John 15:26; 16:14). All who have experienced regeneration owe that experience to the Holy Spirit as well as to the Son of God (Titus 3:5). Israel will be saved just as any Gentile is saved — by grace, through faith in the Lord Jesus Christ, and by the power of the Holy Spirit. Israel's salvation will come through a great spiritual awakening.

The prophet Zechariah envisioned this outpouring of the Holy Spirit in relation to restored and regenerated Israel. "And I will pour upon the house of David, and upon the inhabitants of Jerusalem, the spirit of grace and of supplications: and they shall look upon me whom they have pierced . . ." (12:10). Here is foretold that glorious movement of the Holy Spirit in behalf of the spiritual needs of the remnant preserved in the Tribulation. What a prophecy! National regathering, national restoration, national repentance, and national regeneration.

THE HOLY SPIRIT IN THE MILLENNIUM

The most glorious age of all human history will be the Millennium. When it begins, all who have been redeemed will be a part of it. Then shall be realized that familiar prayer request, "Thy kingdom come. Thy will be done in earth, as it is in heaven" (Matt. 6:10). This will be the golden age, the utopia for which the human race has longed and looked. Numerous prophecies in the Old Testament glow with vivid descriptions of this coming period of time; but the temptation to explore those magnificent word pictures must be by-passed for the present. Our purpose here is to give consideration to the Holy Spirit's activity during the millennial age.

While it is true that all who will enter the Millennium are saved, it is equally true that those believers, being in a natural body, will beget children. Jeremiah speaks of "their children" (30:20). Ezekiel writes about the children who will be born at that time and about their inheritance (47:22, 23). It follows that the children born at that time will be in need of salvation. Apart from the power of the Holy Spirit, there cannot be the salvation experience; in every dispensation, the new birth is effected by the Holy Spirit.

Just as the Holy Spirit descended upon Christ at the beginning of His public ministry at His first advent (Matt. 3:16), even so will the Spirit "rest upon Him" when He reigns at His second advent (Isa. 11:2). In this Isaiah passage, which refers to the coming reign of Christ, all three persons in the Trinity are mentioned. "The Spirit of Jehovah" is the Holy Spirit; the work of salvation during the Millennium cannot be separated from the presence and power of the Holy Spirit.

Isaiah cites another instance of the Spirit's future ministry: "When the enemy shall come in like a flood, the spirit of the LORD shall lift up a standard against him" (59:19). Just as the Holy Spirit restrains the full force of Satan's power in the earth today, so will He do in the kingdom age. He will play a prominent part in the administration of righteousness, preventing all evil forces from assaulting the members of Christ's kingdom. The Holy Spirit will put to flight the enemies of peace and righteousness. The prophet stated earlier that the kingdom blessing cannot be experienced "until the spirit be poured upon us from on high" (Isa. 32:14, 15). God said, "I will pour my spirit upon thy seed, and my blessing upon thine offspring" (Isa. 44:3).

When Isaiah depicted the blessings of the coming kingdom, he said of the king, "And the spirit of the LORD shall rest upon him, the spirit of wisdom and understanding, the spirit of counsel and might, the spirit of knowledge; . . . for the earth shall be full of the knowledge of the LORD, as the waters cover the sea" (11:2, 9). The phrase "as the waters cover the sea" symbolizes the depth and fullness of the knowledge of God on the earth during the Millennium. We know from the teaching of Christ that it is the specialized ministry of the Holy Spirit to search out divine truth and make it plain to man. Jesus said, "He shall teach you all things"

(John 14:26); "He will guide you into all truth" (John 16:13). Paul said, "God hath revealed them unto us by his Spirit: for the Spirit searcheth all things, yea, the deep things of God" (1 Cor. 2:10).

The teaching ministry of the Holy Spirit is the common property of all believers in every dispensation, and the Millennium will be no exception. The full and complete knowledge of God is within the power of the Holy Spirit to impart to God's redeemed children. We need the divine Teacher now, and man will need Him in the dispensations which lie ahead. The subjects of Christ's kingdom will be brought into full knowledge in that day.

It is evident from these passages that the Spirit of God will have a large ministry in the divine program in the future. How we praise God for His presence in the world today! And what a bright prospect for many on earth even after Christ has come to take His church to heaven

Study Questions

1. How is the term *restrainer* to be understood in 2 Thessalonians 2:7, 8?
2. What is the Holy Spirit's role during the Tribulation?
3. What is the Holy Spirit's role in the Millennium?